ONE STEP AT A TIME

STEVE BASS

Written by Steve Bass
Edited by Sow The Seed Ministries and Brad Bass
Cover design and photography by Brad Bass

Manufactured and printed in United States of America

ISBN: 978-0-9915465-0-3

Published by Sow The Seed Ministries
White House, TN

All proceeds from the sale of this book fund the Bass Foundation for Charities, a 501(c)(3) non-profit organization focused on giving back to charities in our community.

To see a full list of our current charities, or to make a donation, please visit www.bassfoundation.org

BASS FOUNDATION *for charities*

CONTENTS

INTRODUCTION

"Hi, I'm Steve Bass from Bass Tire."

Every television ad always started with that introduction. When I first meet someone, I always greet them by saying, "Hi, I'm Steve Bass." I thought it was only fitting to begin my book that way. My friends and customers know that.

Those of you I am just now meeting through my book, I thought that to be a good introduction. As of starting this book I have enjoyed doing business on Nolensville Road, in Nashville Tennessee for over thirty-five years. In that time I have seen business change; I have seen customers change, but the biggest change has been in me. It has taken me thirty-five years to go two miles. This book is about that incredible journey.

Small business is the backbone of our great nation. If you are thinking about becoming an entrepreneur, I want you to read my book. If you manage a business, I want you to read my book. If you have had challenges with finances, church or addictions, I want you to read my book. If you enjoy stories, need encouragement, or just want to smile, laugh or even cry a little, I want you to read my book.

The title of this book is *One Step at a Time.* My friend Richard Walton used to say that you should tackle a large task by doing a little at a time. Charles Dyke, another friend and customer, owns a company in Nashville that installs smart wiring and media components for homes and businesses. Every time I see him and ask how he is doing, he always says the same thing, "A little at a time." Business is built the same way, and so are our lives. You see, the phrases "a little at a time" or "one step at a time" both have the same meaning. Our journeys in life are completed one step at a time.

My book contains many sayings and stories that my customers and friends have shared with me over the years. These sayings and stories have had a great influence on my life, and business. The positive influence has helped my dreams come true. I try to learn from my interaction with people, Use the good, and learn from the bad. My ultimate goal in sharing my story with you is my hope that you can learn from it in some way.

Business lessons, life lessons, and Biblical lessons are all learned a little at a time. If The Lord gave them all to us at one time we could not handle it.

For the past few years I have been honored to speak to a few business groups, usually on the topic of customer service. In business nothing is more important than good old customer service. While speaking to these groups, I generally tell some stories that my customers and friends have found entertaining or meaningful in some way. For the longest time folks have told me, "Steve, you need to write a book." Well, here it is.

I would like to dedicate this book to my late parents, my brother and sisters, my darling wife Kim, and our two children, Charlie and Bradley. I would also like to dedicate this book to our beautiful granddaughter Langley Grace, our fine looking grandson, Luke, Miss Kim's mother and father, Steve and Mary Sills, the late Debbie Oldham, Langley's maternal grandmother, and all my customers and friends. Without family and friends to mold and shape my life, I wouldn't have anything to share with you.

If there are any profits from the sale of my book, I will start a foundation to continue to fund over thirty charities Miss Kim and I contribute to each year.

I would like to give a special thank you to Dr. Gene Mims, our pastor, and his lovely wife Ann for always being an encourager and helping me with the publishing of my story.

Well, here we go!

THE EARLY YEARS

A miserable rainy day in early May 1978 was my first day as store manager for Universal Tire in Nashville. I was so excited. At age 19, all I could think was that I was going to be the best store manager Universal Tire ever had. I had huge dreams for that little store. We opened at 7:30 a.m., which is still my opening time at Bass Tire, but I ran into a little trouble on the way to work. It was pouring down rain and I don't mean maybe.

There is a major intersection two blocks north of my new assignment. At the time, I drove a 1972 Chevy Malibu that my mom and dad helped me buy in high school. When I drove through that intersection, at Thompson lane and Nolensville Road, the standing water on the road flooded my distributer cap, and my car died. At about 8 o'clock, I pulled in to work riding shotgun in a tow truck. I was late, wet, and had spent all my money on the wrecker. Our old mechanic Dave shook his head and told me I sure was off to a bad start. I just didn't know how bad.

Dave said that he thought I was transferred from the main location downtown to close the Nolensville

Road store because of its weak sales volume. But due to low overhead and my youthful energy, maybe I could grow the store. If not, they could pull the plug without much risk to the company. I was facing added challenges to an already difficult task. We had three employees, including me. I would sell a set of tires. Our tire changer David would put them on, and Dave would balance them, sometimes do an alignment, and occasionally a brake job or a set of shocks. I would bill the customer, and then we might go two hours without a phone call or someone walking through the door. This pace was much different than the environment I had become used to at the main store.

The main store environment didn't suit me very well at the time either. I was young, with only a high school education, and had never traveled very far from Dickson. I had a lot to learn. No wonder they sent me to Nolensville Road. I bet I drove my boss crazy.

It was sink or swim time. I called my staff together after a few weeks and let them know if we were going to save our jobs, we had a lot of work to do. So we got busy. Our customers quickly began to see a difference in the way we were doing things. Business began to grow as customers told their friends and neighbors about the good service they received, and our little store took off.

In the first few weeks, I would sell a set of tires and go outside to help install them. After a few months, our shop had grown enough to catch the attention of the main office downtown. We hired an additional tire changer, so I could concentrate on sales and customers. Then we began to request additional equipment. At first we received only hand-me-downs, but as our numbers grew, it became easier to get good equipment. The mechanic's salary began to grow due to rising sales and increased productivity, since his pay structure was base salary plus commission on labor. We still pay our mechanics that way today. We began to request pay raises for our two tire changers. We were well on our way. By year's end, our little store had surpassed all our sales quotas and won store of the year. Our stock and pride level as a team went way up. All my staff received pay increases, and I went to Hawaii.

After four months as manager, when I was still helping with tire installation, I attended my first managers meeting. The meeting was held at the main store, in room 16. Room 16 was a conference room built in the corner of our huge warehouse. It had a conference table, a bar, and a bathroom, and could have easily been used as an apartment. I showed up after work wearing dirty coveralls. I'm sure I smelled a little of rubber and sweat. Every large store manager and company officer had on suits and ties. I can remember feeling out of place and embarrassed. I was seated between Mr. Lovell and Mr. Pate. I can remember how kind those two were to me. I probably embarrassed the president by coming to my first meeting looking like that, but he too, was a gentleman and introduced me as a new manager. He was proud of my hard work, and the fact that I was doing whatever was necessary to give our customers the best service possible.

Most of the meeting was geared toward large truck and commercial business. When it came time to review financial statements and write down what we thought our gross profits should be, I felt like I was in over my head.

I never attended another managers meeting without a coat and tie. Mr. Ed Williams was one of our company comptrollers, and he was kind enough to help me learn to read financials. Universal Tire was the largest independent tire dealer in Tennessee. It was an honor to work for such a good company for ten years. The last two years I worked for Universal Tire, I managed all the Nashville retail stores–quite a climb from that first managers meeting.

During the summer of 2011, I was asked to join the board of trustees for a local hospital. I felt so honored and humbled. I always try my best to slip out a little early from work to grab a quick shower and put on a starched shirt and tie before our monthly board meetings at the hospital. Every time I walked through the administrative offices to the conference room, I thought of my first managers meeting wearing those coveralls. I ran a little late at the store for one board meeting and did not have time to change clothes. I went wearing my Michelin work shirt. The chairman of the board said, "What do you say Michelin Man?" The doctors and other board members I serve with are also attending after work. It doesn't matter to them what I wear, but I always remember the coveralls.

The following year after winning the store contest, manager of year, and returning from Hawaii, my on-the-job training took some strange turns. My tire changer David left to take a manager's job at a competing store. I was very proud of David. I think he thought that if I could manage a store, why couldn't he? But my team was no longer the same. I had to learn about the hiring process.

After a few weeks we hired another tire changer, and I started coaching all over again. In order to have a great team and staff, you have to be like a good coach. Lead by example, coach 'em up, and work them hard. If you love your customers, and work hard, you will be successful.

The next bump in the road with personnel was Dave, my aging front-end mechanic. He realized that with business increasing daily, he was no longer able to keep up. The job was taking a toll on him physically. He resigned to take a less demanding job with his nephew who was in the service station business. Dave was a crusty old fellow that would best be described as a diamond in the rough—a dirty, hard exterior with a big beautiful diamond on the inside. He sure taught me a lot about the tire business, but also about people and life. We formed a friendship that meant so much to me. Dave knew that I didn't attend college, and I worried about my abilities and my future.

On Dave's last day, he told me that he was proud of his four girls. One was a civil engineer, and he told me of her accomplishments. Another one of his other daughters was a school teacher. He told me I was as smart as they were and advised me to never give up and to always work my hardest. If I did that, I would never have to worry about my career. I always treasured his encouragement and kindness. I learned so much from him in a short period of time. He died a few years later, and his funeral procession came past the store. We had a wreath and sign on marquis reading, "We will miss you Dave! Thanks for the memories." That was my first experience with the loss of an employee through death.

Even though he had resigned, he still felt like a current employee. He was my friend.

Early on I formed friendships and built relationships with my customers that have lasted all these years. My first six months with Universal Tire was at the main store. One of my first customers is still with me today. His name is Charles Adams. His family owned a saddle shop around the corner from 12th Avenue and Demonbreun Street. He liked to hunt and fish, so we hit it right off. He has referred all his friends, co-workers and family members to me for tires, and that means so much to me. I mention him because that loyalty is what helped make my company the success I enjoy today.

One of my favorite stories about Charles is about an old Ford pickup truck he had that the king pins were worn out on. I referred him to our Universal Tire truck alignment shop to have them replaced. He is very mechanical and told me he could do them himself. I warned him to be careful with those things. A month or so went by and he came by the store with a broken jaw. "Darn Charles," I said, "have you and Ronnie been fighting?" "No," he replied. "The crow bar slipped while I was changing the king pins and broke my jaw." He always took my advice after that. Ronnie was our postman, and also a good friend to Charles and me until he died a few years later. I have other Charles and Ronnie stories, but I won't tell all of them in my first book. Charles is my longest customer. That is very special to me.

In the coming chapters I would like to tell about some of the famous people I have had the pleasure to wait on. But I must tell you now about a man that I met in the early years, and what an impact he made on my life.

I had been on Nolensville Road for about two weeks, and this guy walked in wearing flip flops, shorts and a T-shirt. He didn't have much hair. His voice carried through the office and into the shop. Dave introduced him to me. His name was Harold Weakley. Now of course I did not have a clue who he was, nor the lessons I would learn from him.

Harold had many talents. When I met him, he was a drummer at the Grand Ole Opry. He had an incredible voice and did a lot of radio commercials. He had worked as a machinist for O'Brien Manufacturing, makers of Duck Head overalls. Harold kind of fell into the music business. Harold was married and had three boys and a daughter. To my knowledge, Harold never drank a can of beer in his life. But one night he was hanging out at Tootsie's Orchid Lounge. He was dating Tootsie's daughter Ann. Tootsie had an act playing at her establishment by the name of Big Jeff. Big Jeff was a local artist, and he was pretty hot at that time. Big Jeff's drummer laid out one night, and he convinced Harold to sit in. He told Harold to chew gum to keep time and it would come pretty easily to him. Boy, was Big Jeff right! Harold joined the musicians union and quickly became a highly sought after session player. He joined the staff band on the Grand Ole Opry, started doing voiceover work, released a record, and became one of the most respected members of the Nashville music community.

I may have learned how to tell stories and entertain people from Harold, but I wasn't born with the music in me. Harold would let me come backstage at the Opry. I got to meet Roy Acuff and listen to music in his dressing room. Many of the artists and musicians became my customers too, thanks to Harold.

Harold wore a hairpiece when he was working. One night at the Opry House, the air conditioning wasn't working, and everyone couldn't wait for the show to end so they could go to Shoney's and eat as they often did. The big group of hungry players got there, and the door to the restaurant was propped open, since their air conditioning wasn't working either. Harold was seated next to Bud Wendell, then manager of the Grand Ole Opry. Harold told Bud if they didn't get some air stirring, he was going to pull off his hairpiece. Bud had never seen Harold without it. When Harold pulled it off, Bud just about crawled under the table. It was so funny. Harold's entire life was like that. He was the kind of guy that made you feel better after being with him. If you

Me with Jimmy Pickel and Charlie at Universal Tire

were down when he came in, you were up by the time he left. Harold has since gone on to be with the Lord, but the beautiful lessons of life he left behind are priceless.

The two fellows I sat between in my first manager's meeting were Mr. Walter Lovell and Mr. Bill Pate, Sr. Both have passed on now, but what an impact those men had on my early years with Universal. Mr. Lovell was vice president of operations and Mr. Pate was the Chattanooga store manager. Both were always willing to help with advice and encouragement. They were busy and important men in our company, but took interest in my career and never made me feel inferior. The president and principal owner of Universal Tire was Mr. Jimmy Pickel, Jr. I learned a lot from Mr. Pickel about how hard he worked and why he expected so much from his management team. I think some of the mistakes I made early on must have driven him nuts. Great customer service was what he was all about. He believed if we did the right thing, maintained a good store image, excellent service, and if we were honest, sales and profits would take care of themselves. He was right then and this philosophy still works today. In my last two years at Universal, I learned how committed Mr. Pickel was to customer service. As the Nashville retail manager, part of my job was to resolve any store or customer service issues. I pretty much had a free hand to spend what was needed, to resolve any issues with our customers. He talked the talk and walked the walk.

It is also important to figure out who signs the checks and make friends with them, too. At Universal, that was Mr. Gene Steakley. He was vice president and treasurer of the company. What a gentleman he was. I won my first trip to Hawaii at age 20, but didn't have any spending money to take on the trip. Mr. Steakley advanced money against commissions earned so I would have spending money on my trip.

Two years later we won the store contest again. Mr. Steakley went with us on that trip to Mexico. The group had dinner one night at one of the top ten restaurants in the world. This place was fancy. Mr. Steakley's wife Betty taught me about table etiquette, salad forks and so on. Mrs. Steakley had the special gift of teaching me during dinner without making me feel inferior. Betty has passed on now, but I will always remember her for that night in Acapulco.

Mr. Steakley always made it easy to discuss business and other things I didn't quite understand, and for that I will always be appreciative. Mr. Steakley and I remain friends and talk on a regular basis today.

Mr. Billy Derryberry was vice president of commercial tire sales. He always treated everyone like family. I never worked in his division, but I think he was instrumental in getting me hired at Universal to begin with. You see, six months before getting hired for a retail sales position, I interviewed with Mr. Derryberry twice for commercial positions. I nearly worried that man to death. I'm sure he asked Wayne Washburn and Jimmy Pickel to hire me so he could get some work done. The lesson learned from Mr. Derryberry is to never give up.

After Wayne Washburn left our company, Universal hired John Morgan. John was my boss and became vice president of sales. I learned a lot from John. We remain very close today. Mr. Morgan and his wife Chris sure had a positive effect on my life. It wasn't until I was older and running my own company that I realized some of the valuable lessons I learned from John. He had been a standout athlete growing up in South Nashville, so he was well known in our community. John had served in the Air Force. He managed stores for Firestone and worked his way to upper management with them. John really knew the tire business. More importantly than that, he knew people. John had the best customer service skills I had ever seen. He knew how to make the customer feel special. He was a marketer. Universal Tire had their name printed on key tags, license plates, golf shirts, buttons and other items like that, and John made sure they got in the customers' hands somehow. Customers liked to get something, and John loved to give it to them. When John came to work at the retail store, it was like a P.T. Barnum circus—the greatest show on earth.

A few years ago, Kim and I helped with the youth in the little church we were attending. Some of the kids didn't have much. Our friend Randy Hodges and his wife, who I'll tell you about later, and Kim and I would

Me and Aaron in our current shop

see that the church kids always had a nice Christmas. When John and Chris Morgan heard what we were doing, gifts for our fall festival fundraiser started to pour in. They sent many expensive items to help raise funds for our youth. They sent personal checks designated for church kids. John has an incredible heart of service that I talk about anytime I speak to a group.

Recently at our current church, Judson Baptist, we had a men's night. We ate dinner and listened to a guest speaker who came to share his testimony. The speaker was retired United States Army Lieutenant General Jerry Boykin. General Boykin was an original member of Delta Force and eventually served as the commanding General of the U.S. Army Special Forces Command at Fort Bragg, North Carolina. David Blair, a good friend of John Morgan's, asked John to attend. After dinner, we filed into the church auditorium and waited for the general to speak. I was seated between John and Aaron who is my store manager at the shop. I thought to myself, "What a great night!" My mentor who helped me so much with my career is seated to my left, and to my right is a young understudy that I have had the honor to help with his career. Quite possibly these two men, one older, one younger, have helped my company grow more than they will ever know. John taught me many lessons, and I have taught those same lessons to Aaron.

When I graduated high school in May of 1976, I had a job lined up at the farmers' co-op. I was going to be a department floater and learn how to sell feed and

My senior picture, 1976

fertilizer. To this day I have never sold a grain. On my first day on the job, someone in the tire shop didn't show up, and I was asked to fill in. That is how I got in the tire business. Kind of like my friend Harold Weakley; I just fumbled into it. Throughout high school I worked in a grocery store. I had no mechanical knowledge nor had I ever changed a tire in my life. It came to me pretty easily, but I had a lot to learn.

The car care center at the co-op in Dickson was a great place to start. We pumped gas, sold tires, did light auto service, all of which was a new and exciting challenge to me. We would get a load of tires in at the railroad station and unload the boxcar into a big dump truck. Then we used pallets and a forklift to put the tires in the racks at the co-op warehouse. All this was done at night after working all day in the shop. Getting overtime was really important in those days when I only earned $2.50 per hour. Looking back I think youth is a good thing: only young people can work that hard.

The co-op sent me to training schools to teach me about the construction of tires. They also sent me to sales seminars. I was just like a sponge trying to soak up all the knowledge I could. I worked my way from the shop to the front office at the co-op. I pumped gas, waited on customers and honed my sales skills. I knew then that this was my calling. I felt like it was time to set my sights on coming to the city to work. I looked in the Yellow Pages to find out the biggest tire dealers in Nashville. I applied at an independent Goodyear store, Universal Tire, Sherling Tire, and a furniture store.

I knew then that this was my calling.

My first contact at Universal, as I mentioned before, was Billy Derryberry. My persistence with him paid off. I was finally hired in November 1977. I was so proud to get the job, I didn't even ask about the salary.

I spent my first six months at the main store in downtown Nashville. I drove back and forth from Dickson, since I still lived at home with my parents. It was a pretty awkward time. I had come from a rural setting to a city atmosphere; from waiting on farmers to trying to wait on business and professional people. At the co-op I was used to putting tires on Chevrolets, Fords, and Chryslers. The city business clientele drove BMWs, Mercedes, Cadillac, Citron, Saab, Renault, and Lincolns. Boy, was I challenged! The competition from our other salesmen was fierce. I had a hard time adjusting to the system and a hard time closing a sale.

Our credit manager's office was up front, close to the sales counter. He had a bird's eye view of the flow of business. After watching me struggle the first month, he called me into his office to have a talk and offer some advice. He had been a Western Auto store manager early in his career, so he knew the ins and outs of that type of sales environment. He observed that when I was with a customer and was about to close the sale, I would really shine. But afterwards I was lost. It was like I became invisible to everyone in the building. I didn't think all the other employees were that busy not to speak or find time to get to know me. He taught me how to become outgoing and initiate conversation with fellow employees. I knew how to do all those things, I was just afraid of saying or doing the wrong thing which might show them I didn't have much education. I was worried I might look dumb. You see the same skills I was using to wait on customers also worked with co-workers. I knew that, I just wasn't using them.

If you are not making a few mistakes, you are not doing enough!

Soon I got into a rhythm. Sales started getting easier, and I became super competitive with the other salesmen. To get my share of customers, I learned how to schedule my work and learned the importance of knowing what the other salesmen had going on. That helped me schedule my customers for service. I still made mistakes, but if you are not making a few mistakes you are not learning or doing enough. I'm sure some of the mistakes I made drove my bosses nuts. I think that is part of the reason why I was sent to the store on Nolensville Road which was the best thing that could have possibly happened to me. You see the Lord was guiding my steps then, I just didn't know it.

If you are not making a few mistakes, you are not doing enough!

THE YOUNGEST OF FIVE

I was born on May 22, 1958, two months pre-mature. I weighed three pounds five ounces and was delivered by Dr. Jimmy Hayes, who I met after I was grown. The odds were against a preemie in those days, but my mother paid no attention to that. She insisted on adding sugar water to my IVs, and my weight climbed. Mothers are usually right. I was the youngest of five children born to T.L. and Myrtle Bass. Now they had two boys and three girls. My brother Tom is the oldest, Linda is the next oldest, then Brenda. The sister eight years older than me is Mitzie.

Seated: Tommy, Dad and Mom. Standing: Mitzie, Brenda, and Linda.

The older three siblings are retired and enjoying the fruits of their labor. Mitzie works with seniors in the healthcare industry in Texas. Tom is retired from the tile business and also from his second job as a coin dealer. One of the last jobs Tom did was to tile the sales office when I built our current store. Today he enjoys traveling, seeing things he never had time for before retirement. Every few weeks I talk to him to find out where he has been and where he is going.

My sister Linda retired from Square D, a company that makes electrical components. She enjoys traveling, taking trips with our sister Brenda, and spending time with her children and grandchildren. Brenda retired from Whirlpool Corporation. She also enjoys traveling with

Linda, Brenda, Mitzie, Tom and myself

Linda and being with her children and grandchildren. Brenda is an avid turkey hunter. Mitzie still lives in Texas. Tom lives about forty miles west of Nashville in our hometown of Dickson. Linda and Brenda live about forty miles southeast of Nashville in Murfreesboro and Woodbury, respectively. Being the youngest, they all say they spoiled me.

When Tom was less than three years old, Pearl Harbor was bombed and dad joined the Navy. He was sent to the South Pacific and stationed at Pearl Harbor on a minesweeper. After the war Dad became an electrical lineman. He traveled stringing power lines. My mother was pretty much a stay-at-home mom with a part time job at a department store. When we moved to Dickson in 1964, she took a job with Red Kap Industries, where she made work clothes. Dad worked for Dickson Electric Department, until his retirement in 1980.

When we moved to Dickson, Tom, Linda and Brenda were all married and had left home. It was just Mom, Dad, Mitzie and me. Mitzie soon married a boy in the Air Force and moved to Japan in 1967. I was nine years old, so it was as if I was an only child until I was grown. All of us are as close as we can be due to the demands of life, but we talk on the phone and visit when possible.

I was 13 when I got my first job at a grocery store. The man I worked for was the most overbearing guy you could imagine. His aunt was nice and the other workers were nice, but that guy was something else. What he taught me was not to be like that. I won't bore you with all the details, but I think you need to know how not to treat a young intern or any other worker.

In 1971, before the mega grocery stores took over, downtown America was thriving in Dickson, as I'm sure it was throughout the rest of the country. Small independent Mom and Pop grocery stores were prominent. There were four on Main Street in Dickson at that time. Most of the stores were laid out the same. There were two display windows on each side of the front doors and two checkout counters at the front. The butcher and meat counter was located in the back of store in front of the stockroom. The dairy case was in the right corner, produce on the left, frozen food adjacent to meat counter, and other groceries were in the middle of store.

This store had an upstairs stockroom as well. You would go out the front door, turn left at the first door, and climb a narrow flight of 25-30 steps to reach the stockroom. There were shelves stocked with items much like those downstairs. When we got caught up with business at the store, we would replenish shelves downstairs with items from upstairs. It seemed like I climbed those steps a hundred times a day. I got the job in the summer. The store hours were 7:00 a.m. to 8:00 p.m., Monday through Friday, 7:00 a.m. to 9:00 p.m. on Saturday and closed on Sunday. For a little chubby kid working over 75 hours a week sacking groceries, taking them to the cars, helping with home delivery, unloading delivery trucks and stocking items, the job was quite an assignment. The manager gave me no time to rest and talked to me in a way that I had never been talked to before.

Before that job I had always spent a couple of weeks each summer with my grandparents in Waverly, Tennessee. I asked my boss for a couple of days off before school started so I could spend a little time with my grandparents and he let me know that school boys didn't get time off or vacations. He used some derogatory language when he told me, and that's when I took that dirty apron off and quit. I told him I would come back on Saturday to pick up my paycheck.

I walked across the street and got a job at Jack Sack and Pack Grocery Store, and I worked there until I graduated high school. Brigham Rumsey was the finest man a kid could ever work for. I didn't ask him about salary, but it was about half of what I was making and worth every bit of it.

I learned so much from Mr. Rumsey. The community loved him. Back in those days, some people would charge their groceries. He would even let some people charge knowing they would never pay him back, but he never let anyone go hungry. It never bothered him to give things away, but it did hurt his feelings when some went to the chain grocery store in Dickson and didn't patronize him after he had been so good to them.

We will talk a little more about credit and loyalty in one of the following chapters. I can remember one lady had a charge account and she often stole from the store. Mr. Rumsey asked me to discretely follow her and let him know what she swiped, and he added it to her bill. She never knew it and paid for it any way. He explained that it was better to handle it that way and not embarrass her or create any more problems for her than she already had.

I can remember one guy asking me where I worked and when I told him, he said some ugly things about my boss. He said he wished he had the money that Mr. Rumsey had added to the scales when he weighed a head of cabbage. I let him know how kind and honest

Mr. Rumsey was and about how many people he gave groceries to, only asking for their business when times got better.

Sometimes a good businessman will work with his heart and not his head. That isn't all bad either. I wished that the guy who had said those things about Mr. Rumsey had that money he was talking about, because he would be broke. I did learn something from that guy that still happens today. Some people talk about things that are untrue. They have no facts, just a desire to tear down and belittle someone else.

Mr. Rumsey died a few years ago and Kim and I went to his wake. There were former sack boys like me there, but not as many people as I had expected. His son Mick told me his dad told him one of the bad things about living so long is that you outlive most of your friends and no one is left to come to your funeral. I guess he was right. He was in his nineties. Mick said he had found a set of books from about a 20-year period before his dad's retirement. There were several hundreds of thousands of dollars' worth of groceries his dad never collected. That amount probably exceeded his net worth at the time of his death.

I wrote a paper in high school about being a business owner. I thought I would have been in the grocery business. When Mr. Rumsey retired he offered to set me up in the grocery business. I declined the offer since I had already started a career in tire business at Universal. I anticipated that the large chain stores would dry up small downtown businesses, particularly small grocers. That actually happened. There again the Lord guided my steps.

I met Lindell Carroll, a route supervisor for Beaman Pepsi, while I was working at the grocery store. I had no idea what an impact we would have on each other's lives in the years to come. Mr. Carroll is an outgoing fellow, and we hit it off right away. When I came to work at Universal Tire, Beaman Pepsi was one of our commercial accounts. They did their business downtown at the main branch. One day after Mr. Carroll had moved to upper management at Beaman, he stopped by the store to purchase some tires for his personal car. After that he started sending all the Beaman company cars and small trucks to my store instead of the main store. That was just what my store needed to help us turn the store around. I always thanked Mr. Carroll for being such an important part of my early career.

When Beaman sold to Pepsico, Mr. Carroll bought a service station on Nolensville Road and became a business icon in our community until his retirement. I sent Mr. Carroll a lot of mechanical business through the years to pay him back for helping me so much when I was young and just getting started on Nolensville Road. Our business community is not as good a place since Mr. Carroll retired. We miss him very much. He works hard in his church, and continues to make a difference in people's lives, as he did in mine.

I met two other people as a kid at Jack Sack and Pack that would impact my life later on. Wentworth Caldwell, Sr., an older gentleman who owned a small wholesale grocery warehouse. His son became the president of H.G. Hill Grocery, a well-loved and well-run business in Nashville. H.G. Hill became one of my largest accounts and they bought tires for their tractors, trailers and company cars from me. We still do the vehicles for the realty division for the Hill Co. and Mr. Hill's and Mr. Caldwell's decedents still let us service their tires.

I always said that H.G. Hill had the best and nicest employees, from the warehouse worker all the way to Mr. Hill himself. They had almost no turn over; many of their employees never worked anywhere else, which speaks well for Mr. Hill and his management team. They had a model that businesses could learn from today.

I met a truck driver named Mr. Roberson who worked at C.B. Ragland Company, an independent grocery distributor we purchased from during the sack and pack days. When I came to Nolensville Road, Mr. Roberson bought his tires from me until he died. Jim Ragland is my client today. You never know what impact relationships can make and how they can last a lifetime.

You never know what impact relationships can make and how they can last a lifetime.

Growing up in Dickson was great. Some of the neighborhood boys and myself hung out at the plaza shopping center, went to the movies, rode bikes, built forts, went camping, all the stuff kids in our time did.

As I mentioned earlier, I usually spent a couple of weeks in the summer with my grandparents. My grandfather was a beekeeper. I have fond memories of robbing the beehives and putting the honey in jars. My grandmother made incredible fried pies from dried apples picked from our own apple trees. The only vice Mamma and Papa Bass had was dipping snuff. They never said an ugly word or were unkind to anyone; they lived a simple life. They never had drivers' licenses and never owned a car. They probably never had over $500 at one time in their lives, but their wealth was beyond measure. Papa Bass lived to almost ninety, and Mamma Bass lived to be ninety-nine.

I remember Mamma Bass watching Billy Graham on a black and white Admiral TV. She followed along in her Bible. I also remember her watching wrestling on Saturday afternoons and getting pretty worked up about the matches. Papa Bass took me fishing at the creek and let me help in the garden. Sunday meals and holiday meals at Mamma Bass's were very special. I encourage all young parents to make sure your children spend time with their grandparents and let them pass on the beautiful memories and the lessons of life.

I learned later how important education is.

I did go to work while I was young, and maybe I missed out on some kid stuff, but I wouldn't change a thing. One of my dad's friends was on the board at the co-op, and after high school I got hired. Later on Dad arranged for me to take an exam to go to work for the phone company. Dad, being a lineman, knew the phone company would be a good place to work. No hot power lines and no real high climbing. I told Dad I couldn't climb; I still can't. I was sure I wouldn't past that test.

Some weeks later my dad learned how I did on the test. Dad told me, "Boy, you surely ain't that dumb." "No, Dad," I said. "I told you I would find a job on the ground." He said, "Boy, you will starve to death."

A few years ago I spoke to a group of AT&T employees in downtown Nashville. I shared that experience with them. Had I known that most of the telephone work was going *under*ground, I would have done better on that test and I might have listened to a different speaker with them that day!

In those days, if you had tuition money or student loans, you could go to college, or you could go to work right after high school. I went to work. I learned later how important education is.

THE DREAMS OF BEING A BUSINESS OWNER

A few years went by and I continued to build a good business with the company I managed. I won the store contest again in 1980. I met Miss Kim and got married in 1983. I let her know I had some debt and a young son, but as you know love always prevails, and she wasn't scared at all. I guess Charlie and I were pretty easy to love. Soon I quit my second job and it was full speed ahead. Now I had a helper and partner. Financially

Me and Charlie

Kim, Charlie and Me

we had our struggles, but it was a great time in our lives. I look back now and I wouldn't change a thing.

Times were very lean for us early on. We often took a calculator to the grocery store to keep track of our purchases so we didn't overdraft our account. I can remember the government cheese my folks shared with us. We were lucky to have that cheese so we could make pimento sandwiches. Kim's career in the medical field was on track at Vanderbilt University Medical Center. My career was also strong at Universal. In 1987, the Lord blessed us with another son, Jonathan Bradley Bass. We bought a house in Nashville, trimmed the fat from our household budget, sold our new car and bought a used car for a lower payment, so that Kim could be a stay at home Mom.

Kim and Bradley

Charlie entertaining Bradley during his first Christmas in 1987

We learned early on how to live on less and how to prioritize for what was really important. We still practice that today. We are not tight, but we don't waste either. I have the first dollar Bass Tire ever made framed in my office. I still remember where it came from and what she had to say about money. The lady's name was Ms. Walker. She worked at Clover Bottom for the state of Tennessee. I don't guess she ever made a lot of money, but she always had what she needed. Ms. Walker said, "It's not what you make, it's what you take care of," I have never forgotten those words.

By 1987 I ran the Nashville branch of retail stores for Universal, and mine were doing well. We even built a new store on Nolensville Road in 1984. I was working hard, my stores were profitable, and life was good. Early in 1987 a manufacturer's representative asked if I had ever thought about being in business for myself. I had a client who bought an old building on Nolensville Road just down the street, and he asked if I knew anyone who might be interested in renting it. I said, "Yes–me."

"It's not what you make, it's what you take care of"

Bass Tire's original location at 3015 Nolensville Road

He agreed to let me get my affairs in order and held the building for me under the condition that I would do the sweat equity and get it cleaned up and remodeled for my use. I put together a business plan, recruited three employees (not from Universal), got equipment and suppliers lined up, then got turned down by the bank. Another customer, Mr. Fly, agreed to help me with the financing. In November I resigned from Universal Tire after ten years. I turned in my company truck, said my goodbyes, and Bass Tire was born.

This was a scary time in our young family's lives. I was 29 years old with a job, but with no income. Miss Kim was a stay at home mom with no Vanderbilt paycheck. We had a mortgage, very little in savings, and were certainly not in the best position for me to quit my job and start a new company.

I would like to share my thought process concerning that. I was on my game at Universal. Business was smooth with very few snags. My stores were profitable. My staff was stable. I thought if I was going to try to make it on my own, now was the time. That way if I did not make it, maybe I could go back to Universal while I was still young.

We started the clean-up process on the old building I had rented. It was November, and the landlord had given us the first two months rent free in lieu of work on the building. We spent our personal savings in the first two weeks. We lived on our credit cards during December. Opening day was January 3, 1988, and we hit the ground running.

Our new business was on a shoestring budget. The first bank that had turned us down didn't think we could open on that low amount of money. After three months of financials, the bank changed their mind. They loaned us our startup costs and I was able to repay Mr. Fly and become the sole owner. This was good because the profits would be enough for my salary and my employees, but not much room for a silent partner. Mr. Fly continues to come to the office every day, if he is able. He makes coffee and helps answer the phone. We could not have started our company without Mr. Fly, and I will always be thankful to him. His friendship sure has meant the world to me. Mr. Fly is another diamond in the rough.

Mr. Fly chatting with John Carswell and Bill Rundle

When we got started I learned how valuable the support staff from Universal was to me. I didn't have a purchasing department or a warehouse with endless resources. With the previous company, we had an advertising department, human resources, accountants, credit departments, legal staff, and equipment maintenance personnel. I now realize why the financials with Universal always hit me with a management charge. I also realize why the bank first turned me down. I didn't borrow enough money for operating capital. I began to put my company into debt. The expenses out ran my profits. We still struggle with that today. We really have to be careful with our spending.

We started to get behind on 941 payroll taxes, and then we got behind on our sales tax. What a mess. I met with a customer that was a retired IRS agent. At the time he was working for the State of Tennessee at the Department of Revenue. When he came by the store, he was not there to buy tires. He was there to discuss the payment I owed the state for sales tax. I will never forget his words. "Steve, you cannot borrow yourself out of debt." Well that was great advice. I'm so glad I had a friend assigned to my account. He was kind and willing to work with me to get my mess cleaned up, one step at a time. There's that title phrase again. He advised me to pay the next month's sales tax in full when it was due. Then pay on my back taxes until I could catch that up. I did the same thing with the 941 taxes. Upon advice from my accountant, we outsourced our payroll. They gave me the amount each week to stub our checkbook, and I never spent my tax money on anything else, no matter what. It was all electronically filed, and I never got behind again.

Our current bookkeeper, who has been with us many years, took care of our sales tax to keep me from spending that money, too. We never got behind on sales tax again either. It is all electronic now. I just have to make sure funds are available to see that they are paid. That adjustment period really put me behind, but we overcame it.

We also paid on our bank note and had credit lines from the bank. While we were navigating all that, building the business, building our home life, our country slid into a light recession. We went to war with Iraq. That had a negative impact on our business. It impacted our sales just enough to slow our financial growth as a company. Keep in mind we took a very minimal salary. We had an employee making more than we did. This was 1991, the infant stages of our business. Times were still very lean. But our lives had always been lean, so we just never gave up and continued to go to work every day and do our best. We continued to give our customers the best products and service we knew how.

Last year I was honored to be the guest on a local cable television show, Nashville Inner City Ministries. Founder Lytle Thomas, a Church of Christ preacher and my friend, asked me to be his guest. He wanted me to talk about life and give encouragement to young single moms in the inner city who were having a hard time with the daily struggles of life. I know how dedicated Lytle has been in his ministry and what a difference he has made. His success didn't come overnight; just one step at a time.

never, never, never give up.

At the end of the broadcast I shared with Lytle and his viewers a story from the late Winston Churchill. A farmer kept a butter churn with milk in the creek to keep cool. The lid came off and two frogs fell into the milk. One swam around until he got tired, and then he gave up and drowned. The other kept kicking and swimming and fighting. When the farmer came back to the creek to get his milk, he found one dead frog and the other one sitting on top of a big ball of butter. The moral to that story is never, never, never give up. Kim and I have taken that approach to our business and personal life.

In October 1990, I lost my father to cancer. He fought a ten year battle. Dad had two operations early on and had eight good years after that. He began to decline during the last two years. As tough as it was, at least he had time to do things with Mamma, enjoy the grandkids, and wrap up his life here on Earth. Having our mother to see about and make sure she was taken care of made dealing with Dad's death a little easier at the time. We are supposed to celebrate in death, but it sure is hard to do.

About that time I had an offer to liquidate my company and return to Universal to run a store they had bought in nearby Franklin, Tennessee. Management thought I would be a good fit. They agreed to pick up my debt, place most of my employees, and give me a nice compensation package. It sure seemed like a good deal. Kim and I began to talk about it and weigh the options. We prayed that we would make the right decision. But we knew if we gave up now, we would probably never start another business again. So we reevaluated our goals, and talked about why we went in to business in the first place.

Education for our two boys was our primary goal. We always felt like if our business was successful and profitable, we would be able to afford a good education our children. Kim and I wanted to give the boys every advantage we could. Charlie had always been in private school. We intended for Brad to go to private school as well, and wanted college to be an option when the time came. We decided to stay on course with our dream, no matter how challenging it would get. We vowed then that if we didn't make it, it wouldn't be from lack of commitment and hard work. We turned down the opportunity to liquidate. I like to think of it as turning down the opportunity to give up. We made that decision

We vowed then that if we didn't make it, it wouldn't be from lack of commitment and hard work.

and never looked back. The children's education was important to Kim and me. You see, we realized how we wanted the boys to get a college education, something that we did not have.

I always thought we would open multiple locations, like Universal did. In the mid-nineties, finding good personnel was challenging. It seemed to us that all the good workers already had jobs. In order to open more locations, we would have to take on more debt and partners. We decided that since our one store was making us and our employees a decent living, we would just keep plugging along.

Toward the late nineties, we realized we needed to own our own building. That was our next goal. We began to get our bank note and credit lines paid down so we could start the search for a building or property. In 1999 we found some property, secured a construction loan and started getting it done.

Bass Tire's current location at 3801 Nolensville Road

It took thirteen years of doing business and renting to get to this point. But we continued to chip away at our dreams, remembering to practice due diligence and patience, one step at a time. Our business was no longer an infant. It was growing up. As the years go by, your business will constantly change. Some changes you won't like and some will be for the better.

It is my opinion that most entrepreneurs are control freaks. I know I am. We like making decisions, pushing things forward, calling the shots, and being in complete control of our business. So many things happen around us, however, that sometimes we have absolutely no control over the situation, no matter how prepared we are. That still drives me nuts, but I have to realize the Lord is in control and I need to quit worrying about things I can't control.

MISTAKES

Oh boy. This could easily turn into the longest chapter in the book. If I wrote about all the mistakes I have made in life and in business, there wouldn't be enough ink or paper to print them. I am going to share a few of them with you as they come to mind, in no particular order. I am not going to preach to you. Most lessons in life are learned on your own anyway. After all, if I had listened to all the advice my mother gave me, I would have become a multi-millionaire today. But if I can be a positive influence and someone can learn from my mistakes, so be it. I need to write about them. As a rule anything in moderation is generally okay. But for those of us with addictive tendencies, that rule is pretty risky.

I didn't smoke until I was grown. In fact as a young person I was really against smoking. I started fooling around with cigarettes, and the next thing I knew, those things had a hold on me. I always needed a pack. I needed a light. I needed an ashtray. My clothes stunk. My breath stunk. My teeth were stained. My breathing was affected. My truck seats had burn holes in them. On and on with all these problems, but none of that was enough to make me quit. I wanted to but I was addicted. When I asked the Lord to deliver me from them, He did, but it about killed me. Now I have no desire to use tobacco. Not to mention all the money I spent on them and medical bills for the damage they caused. I have heard people say things like, "My uncle smoked three packs a day and lived to be 95." Well he was a luckier man than me.

Drinking got in the way of me being a good witness for the Lord. I never got a DUI or got in trouble with the law, but I did get in trouble with my mother at home when I was young and with Miss Kim later on. No matter where you go, someone is always watching how you conduct yourself. If I continued to do those things, it could have become a negative influence on those who were watching me. Maybe it did, but I am so glad all that is behind me.

I remember going to the grocery store and running into my friend Harry Caldwell. Harry was a school teacher and lived just around the corner from Kim and me. We visited for a while, and he noticed the grocery list in my hand. Harry saw the words "cigs and beer." Harry repeated that line and said, "Steve Bass?" Harry is always an encourager and not one to judge. I didn't think much of it right then, but it hit me later. You see Harry's opinion mattered to me. I respected him so much. I sure didn't want Harry to be disappointed in me.

It seemed in those days, I would always run into someone in public after I had been drinking. Having the smell of just one beer on my breath embarrassed me when I saw someone I didn't expect.

I seem to have an addictive personality. When I was smoking I wanted to smoke them all. If I was eating something I liked, I wanted to eat it all. Drinking was no different. I have learned to control my urges with help from the Lord, and others like Harry, who may not have even known they were influencing me.

It is just best for me to leave smoking and drinking alone. Others have to work out their addictions themselves and I will not judge them, but it is best if I leave it all alone. I felt it was important to share this with others. Everyone has their struggles in life. For some it is gambling, for others it may be drugs, but if I let others know why it was important for me to get a hold on smoking and drinking, I might be able to encourage someone and help them overcome their addictions.

Another mistake I made in my personal life was not being consistent taking my family to church. So many great preachers made a positive impact on my life, but I wasn't ready to give up the stuff that kept me out of church. I sure am glad the Lord and I got that worked out! It was Jesus' custom to go to church, and I am proud to tell you that is my custom, too. Life is hard. Doing business in the proper manner is hard. I told you I was not going to preach, but I will tell you it is easier when you're not doing it alone. If you don't attend a local church, find one. You will have a preacher that cares about you, new friends that care about you, and you will learn to serve the Lord who loves and cares for you. I really regret what I call the wasted years–the years when I wasn't in church.

Business mistakes happen pretty regularly. I stated earlier in the book that if you don't make a few mistakes, you probably aren't doing much. I told you about the tax mistakes I made during the early years of our business and how we corrected that. Now let me tell you about the mistakes I made in the name of advertising. I put our logo on bowling teams, race teams, softball teams, and even fishermen. All these sponsorships were for adults. Let me tell you my thoughts on that and what we do now.

I finally realized I was financing someone else's hobby, when I didn't have a hobby myself. I had just my work and my family. The bowling team I sponsored was pretty good. They won their league. The captain of the team and one other member traded with us, but the advertising didn't make much of an impact on our business. The softball team was phenomenal, but when I quit sponsoring their teams, they started buying their tires somewhere else.

I did a little bit better with the race teams. The nineties were a great time for weekend stock car racing at Nashville's Fairgrounds Speedway. The grandstands were full every Saturday night, and we took the kids almost every week. It was a good low cost entertainment for families.

At one time we sponsored a car in every division. Two cars won track championships flying the Bass Tire colors. Some of the contacts we made with our racing sponsorships continue to do business with us today, even though we no longer sponsor racing.

We bought a motor home and carried employees and customers to NASCAR races. We rented the skybox at the Fairgrounds Speedway to let our employees and their families come watch the races. What a good time we had. We made some great memories, but we were spending too much money on it.

One evening after work, we were doing an alignment on one of our sponsored racecars when a customer dropped by. He walked through the bay door, looked around and asked if that is what we spent our money on. He went on to say no wonder I didn't have any money. I paused and thought, "You are right." Our racing days helped to promote our company, but we never outran what it cost us. I told the mechanic doing the alignment that when he finished, Bass Tire was done with racing. And just like that it was over.

For years, teams continued to approach us for sponsorships. We decided that we would be better served to give to children's charities. When we got a request to put our name on an adult hobby, we offered to make a donation in their name to a charity instead of giving them cash. To this day we have never had any takers. This is how we corrected those mistakes. I will discuss charities and giving in another chapter.

Brad, myself, and Charlie watching a race from the infield

I'm a passionate person, and sometimes in the heat of the moment, I fly off the handle. Sometimes I have been guilty of getting loud with suppliers, employees, and even a little loud with customers. Well, for a guy that has built a business on cool temperament, calmness and being the best at customer service, I am just plain ashamed to have ever made that mistake.

In your business there may be a supplier or vendor you may have to stand your ground with. Occasionally, there will be a coworker you have to be firm with. Keep your cool. I destroyed a relationship with an insurance supplier once when I pushed him a little too far when I thought I was being mishandled. I have since made my apologies and changed agents twice, but that has always bothered me because regardless of whether or not he treated me unfairly, I had no excuse to handle him the way I did. I should have done what I know to do. I should have been kind, figured out a solution, and hopefully convinced him to compromise.

I have always tried to learn from my mistakes and not make the same mistakes over and over. I heard somewhere that there is no shame in making a mistake; just don't keep making the same mistakes. I was on a committee at a church we once attended, and I was facing a tough decision. I sought advice from Lee Brown, from the Fellowship of Christian Athletes. He said, "Whatever you do, do it with love." Every time I mess up I think of that phrase. I'd like to remember that first, before I mess up.

One of our former presidents was asked what mistakes he thought he made during his presidency. He couldn't think of any. Well I have been a little more honest with you—and I really liked that president!

If there is anyone on your mind and you feel like letting them know you love them, let them know. You may not get another chance. One afternoon I was busy on the phone and one of my friends, Stan Lyell came by the shop to pay his bill. I saw him, waved and kept doing what I was doing. The next morning he had a heart attack. He was gone. Had I known that day was the last time I was going to see him, I would have hung up the phone, hugged him and told him how much I loved him.

Another mistake I have made in business feeling like I have to be in direct control of all aspects of the store. It's probably time for me to get off the sales floor on a daily basis and start letting my staff take care of the day-to-day business. I think I have held my staff back, and it is probably time to let go some.

I don't think I have done as good a job balancing my time as I should have. In the name of building our business, too much of my time was spent at work and not quite enough was spent with Kim and the boys.

I have spent a little too much time worrying about the future. Will we have enough funds to retire and enjoy a comfortable lifestyle? Will we be able to give money away? I now think that all that concern was a mistake.

Be careful with credit. It can quickly get out of control. One of my other mistakes is the amount I've had to write off through the years.

CHARITIES AND GIVING

The Bible is pretty clear on tithing ten percent. Offerings are any amount you are led to give above that initial ten percent. A customer we attend church with asked me about giving. She wanted to know if she should tithe on her net or gross earnings. I told her that I interpret it as the first fruits, which to me means gross. She also asked if our business tithed.

I will share my answers to you concerning her questions. Ten percent of net is a good place to start because it is pretty easy to compute. If your total take-home income from all sources is $500, than make your tithe check out for $50. Do it when you stub your book the day you get paid, so on Sunday, the Lord's money is ready. If you miss a Sunday at church, the check is already done and you drop in two checks the next Sunday. Just because you miss attending, don't miss tithing. Once you get going, start increasing your tithe until you get to the gross amount.

There is always something to give to at church, such as building funds, mission trips and other programs. I always make sure Miss Kim hits all of them, that way if we are off a little on our tithe, we will balance out in the Lord's favor.

Our company also joins in. When our church buses and vans needed tires, I made an invoice on the work just like normal, but I didn't charge the church. The church office made out a donation letter for taxes. Donations were also made to our church building fund. These amounts are ten percent of my company's profits through the building time period. I then give to about thirty charities for our offerings.

I think structured giving through your home church is vital. Some people think they can't afford to give. I understand, I used to think that way. It should be a goal to start giving. Get a budget together and see what is costing so much that you think you can't give. Once

Miss Kim's parents, Steve and Mary Sills

you figure that out, you can start to give, even if it's not the whole ten percent.

Watch the blessings from heaven start to flow when you start giving. My father in law once told me "You can't out give the Lord." He was right. Sometimes the blessings are financial, sometimes they are good health, or the opportunity to help someone else. Having the ability to give is just like operating a business, one step at a time.

After my father died, my siblings and I realized that our mother's social security wouldn't quite cover her expenses, and we started sending her a check each month. Between the five of us we never missed the money, and it sure helped her. Miss Kim had an elderly aunt, we also sent a little money to. I feel that it is important to help our own family members as well as others. I can't tell you how good it feels to make a difference.

Having the ability to give is just like operating a business, one step at a time.

Sometimes helping others is not always financial, your time can be just as valuable. A few years ago, I spent a few hours here and there helping a nephew prepare a business plan, sales projections and banking information for a business loan. I helped him get his business started. He did great and has since started a new business on his own. I have given advice to others starting out in business through the years, and consider it an honor to be asked to help.

With today's unstable retirement accounts, it is hard not to worry some. I wonder sometimes if I have given too much away. I wonder if that should have been a part of my Mistakes chapter. After we retire maybe I'll write another book and let you know my findings on that. In the meantime, Kim and I are going to stay the course.

I would like to form a foundation so our thirty or so charities can receive money from now on. If ball players, entertainers and big corporations can do it, why can't I? It might be on a smaller scale, but pennies make dollars.

My friend Jack Wilkerson once told me he thought it would be nice if when the last shovelful of dirt hits your casket, you could have given it all away.

RECESSIONS AND CHALLENGES

My mother died in September 2008, of complications from a broken hip. I'll talk about that difficult time in a coming chapter. In the last few months before her death I was away from the store quite a bit. My siblings and I spent time taking care of her.

One morning before leaving the house, I saw on the news that a big bank had sold some Coke stock to raise capital and shore up their assets. They may have worded it differently, but you get the picture. I felt then that something big was about to happen. Sure enough, it was the beginning of the biggest economic down turn since the Great Depression.

In our twenty-five years in business, we survived the slow economy of the Gulf War in the early 1990s, the terror attacks in New York and Washington in 2001 and the two wars that followed, gas prices hitting an all-time high, and now another recession. People ask if the recession has affected our business. I reply, "If it affects our customers, if affects us." Our business is a little more resilient than other types of businesses. If folks are not buying new cars, they are fixing their old ones. So the tire replacement and repair business is not as hard hit as others. However, if folks are not working, their car is not moving as much, and they don't have the money for repairs.

It is my belief that top notch workers, fair pricing, reliable products, repeat business, and the best customer service available has helped keep our business thriving during challenging times. We have endured big box stores and discount chains, all the challenges with the fuel situation, wars, recessions, and yet we still manage to grow. I am so thankful for all of our loyal customers. I'm also thankful for a great staff that takes pride in their work. That's what makes us shine.

My advice in this economy is to do all the things it takes to build your business. It doesn't matter what business you are in or who you work for. Do your best, give it your all, and be a little better than the competition. If you are the best at what you do, you will make a living and reap rewards from your hard work.

One general problem I see is that many people take shortcuts. If you sow sparingly, I think you will harvest sparingly. It ain't rocket science! Good, old-fashioned service and hard work will work every time. You don't have to be the cheapest guy in town, but you do have to try to be the best. People usually don't remember the price, but they never forget inferior service. No matter how much you cut your prices, somebody will always find a way to sell what you sell cheaper. One of the problems with trying to be the cheapest is that you can't make enough profit to offer the kind of service your customers want. Any business earned on price alone will be lost on price alone.

At the end of the day the customer base that is going to stay with you and be loyal will recognize value.

The little things you do for them as a courtesy that the other guys usually charge for really add up. So many times retailers will use bait and switch tactics. Sometimes they might be a little cheaper up front, but they'll charge you later for another service. We find it is better to just be fair across the board and do what you say you will do.

Once trust is established between you and the customer, they will know you are going to be fair and honest and not charge them for something you didn't do.

Working on a car is kind of like an orthopedic doctor replacing your hip. You have to trust that he uses the right equipment and that your leg won't end up shorter than the other one. You want his staff to be the best at what they do. You usually don't want the cheapest surgeon operating on you. It is all about trust and confidence. Our customers deserve the best and we aim to deliver. That kind of care is what keeps them coming back, not the price. Trust will weather hard times, recessions and challenges.

As a word of encouragement, if your business has survived the great recession thus far, you and your company are doing something right. If the recession has taken your job or cut back your work, always remember this: tough times don't last, but tough people do. Remember what Winston Churchill said about giving up.

I talk about steps. In order to take a step, you have to put one foot down in front of the other. Pick 'em up and lay 'em down. I can remember my dad talking about pick 'em up and lay 'em down. He used that saying talking about football players who could run fast. Now there was a man who knew all about hard work and challenges.

My parents were raised during the Great Depression. Just about the time the country was coming out of the depression, the world went to war. The Navy sent my dad to a minesweeper in the South Pacific. If you don't know, a minesweeper is a ship that has a wooden hull so magnetic mines wouldn't be attracted to it. It

My Mother with Tom and Linda, and Dad in his Navy blues

would clear the water for battleships and destroyers. Can you imagine how those young sailors felt when the chains on that ship would set off one of those mines? I wonder how my mother felt at home, by herself with two young children, wondering if my dad would make it home.

In those days all across our great nation, all families endured hardships and similar challenges. Thanks to my parents and the men and women from those generations, we have something here in America to be so proud of. Knowing what they faced makes our challenges look pretty small. I don't know about you, but I'm not backing down from challenges. I am going to face them head on and overcome. Shoot, I owe so much I don't have any other choice!

AMERICAN MADE

When I think of my parents, I think about how hard my folks worked to give us a better life than they had. When I look through old family photo albums, I see pictures of the cars my folks drove, and now I see some of those same cars on televised auctions. I can't help but think what a golden age that time was for our country. In those days if something wasn't made in America, it was inferior. Now with our global economy, it is hard to buy or sell much that is made in America.

Back in the early nineties, I had the opportunity to fly to North Carolina and visit the largest tire manufacturing plant in the world. That company sent their private plane to pick me up. When we pulled in, my name was on the marquis welcoming me as a visitor to their plant. Boy, I was in tall cotton! By the way they greeted me you would have thought I was the governor.

Besides seeing the building process of the tires and learning as much as I could, what I remember the most was seeing my name on the marquis, and how hard everyone at that plant worked. I didn't know any of them, but it gave me a sense of pride to sell their product. I really dwell on the name thing because everyone likes to see their name somewhere. They also like to be addressed by their name. I do my best to remember people and their name. It is important for them and for me. Every time I sold a tire from that manufacturer, I would tell customers about visiting that plant. I always think a little bragging on someone never hurts anything. That person or group may never hear about it, but you never know. It is a small world.

A couple years ago I had the privilege of visiting the Texas proving grounds for another one of our tire manufacturers. I have a friend in Illinois who works on the production line, building tires for that manufacturer. He is going to school for research and development, and the company is helping with his education expenses. I told him about visiting the proving grounds and how impressed I was with the facility and the staff. It was important to him that I was treated well and that I enjoyed my visit. That company impressed me with the test I put their product through. I told my friend that he might have touched some of the tires I tested.

One of my customers has two boys that I watched grow up. One is a flight nurse on a medical helicopter. You know if a Life Flight chopper has to land between power lines in the road to get you to the hospital, you are probably in bad shape. I wonder how many lives he has helped to save. The other son is the largest employer in his county. He started out painting cars, and eventually landed automotive parts contracts, military contracts, and so forth. He built that tremendous business one step at a time. His workers, I'm sure, buy tires from a local dealer like me. Maybe some built by my friend. God bless him for his hard work to create jobs.

In the 1980s, radial construction in tires was pretty new in America. That technology is probably the biggest innovation in our industry since the tubeless tire. I can remember customers wanting to know where a particular brand of tire was built. Some wanted the ones built in certain foreign countries, not the ones built in the U.S.A. I can remember telling them then that I like the ones built here, and that I had more confidence in our American workers. I believed it then, and I still do.

I can remember telling them then that I like the ones built here, and that I had more confidence in our American workers. I believed it then, and I still do.

In the 1970s my mother went to work in the garment industry. Many small towns in the U.S. at that time had garment factories that produced a lot of jobs. I am saddened that most are gone now. To cut costs, garments are manufactured overseas. I would give an extra $5.00 for a shirt or pair of pants if I knew it was made in America. I saw on TV that some communities are buying made in America Christmas gifts to make a difference. It has to start somewhere. I'm proud to see that.

When you can, buy American built. The worker your purchase helps may be my customer. A lot of Americans take pride in our country. We look out for our neighbors. We don't want the government taking care of us. We just want our elected officials to understand this, too. We need them to do the right thing. By creating jobs and getting a proper tax structure in place, we can start working on reducing the deficit, one step at a time.

I don't how we got in such a mess. I guess one step at a time for that, too. I'd say that if you were to ask what kind of job our folks in Washington are doing, most people would give them a bad grade. I don't know about them, but if I were there, that would bother me. I would want to do something about it. It really doesn't matter to me what party you are in. I am a registered democrat from years ago, but I have voted republican a lot.

I overheard an older customer talking with some other older men one day at my store. One of the guys asked him who he was voting for in the upcoming presidential election. He said, "I'm not for the democrats or the republicans." Then he asked the other fellow what he was for, and he replied, "Social security." I have thought about that statement a lot. If nothing else, it's a funny story to tell, but after thinking about it, I am, too. I'm not necessarily partial to either party, but I'm all for our elected officials doing the right thing. I know we have some great men and women in Washington. But I think some aren't there to help the country as much as they are there to help themselves. My preacher reminded me that it didn't matter who was in the White House, because the Lord is still in control. We can take comfort in that, too.

Another thing while I am on my soapbox here. Nowadays if you don't have a pretty big budget, you can't run a county-wide race and stand much of a chance. I recently called one of our local officials at his office to ask advice on a seat about to become vacant. I asked how much money it would take for me to run a county-wide race in Metro-Davidson County and stand a chance. He said $150,000. Wow! How much would it cost to run for Congress? The point I am making here is that this figure takes the average American workingman out of the picture. If you had that much in your savings, you would not spend it on getting elected. If you held fundraisers, there might be a group to give you enough to get elected, but then you are obligated to vote how they want you to. Oh boy, no wonder it got out of control. It all boils down to doing the right thing.

Former U.S. Congressman Bob Clement is my friend and customer. He told me that when he was in Washington we had a balanced budget. I know he knows a lot, and someday I think I'll ask him what happened. He is a good man that to my knowledge always tried to do the right thing. Our families go back to my home town of Dickson. The congressman's father and my father were friends. Bob's father, Frank Clement, was governor of Tennessee. My dad was a local utility worker and worked hard in his friend's campaign. My dad didn't have a hidden agenda; he knew the man would do a good job, and he supported him. Had Mr. Clement let my dad down, he would have called him out on it. It is not quite that simple today, but the concept is the same.

I enjoy hearing the congressman's stories. Of course he has been to the White House many times. He had dinner with several presidents. I always have a few stories for the congressman, too. Washington would do better if more men like Bob Clement were elected to office. One of Bob's good friends is one of my customers, Butch Garrett. Butch has many boyhood memories and plenty of stories I love to hear. One of my favorites is about Elvis Presley coming to the governor's mansion to sing gospel music with a Tennessee State Penitentiary quartet called the Prisonaires. I guess named after The Jordanaires who sang with Elvis for many years. Elvis sang all night long.

Congressman Clement has many great stories. Another one of my favorites is about when Bob was a teenager living in the governor's mansion. His mom and dad bought him a fast back Ford Mustang, of which he was very proud.

Most of the staff at the governor's mansion were convicts from the state prison. Most were convicted of crimes of passion. Studies would show they made the best workers in that type of environment.

They had a cook named Willie. Willie was the best cook that Bob can remember being assigned to the governor's mansion. When Bob's mom and dad were out of town, Bob thought he was in charge of the executive residence. One time Willie stole Bob's Mustang to go see his girlfriend Francine. When Bob realized that his car was gone, he immediately had the Tennessee Highway Patrol and the Nashville Police Department put out an APB on his car and Willie. Within the hour, Willie and the Mustang were returned, and when asked what to do about Willie, Bob said that he would recommend his father keep Willie on staff. He did tell Willie that if he ever needed to steal a car again to go see Francine, to steal his mom and dad's car!

Our country needs more people like Bob Clement and his wife Mary. They both have a passion to serve and do the right thing. This great Tennessee family has done so much for the state and the entire country. Kim and I are very proud to call the Clements our friends.

I mentioned Bob's good friend Butch Garrett. The Garrett family sure has meant a lot to me. Not only have the Garrett's served in some of our local government offices, they were in the drug store business. They helped many young people get educated and become pharmacists.

One such man is Wade Wilson. Wade owned the Garrett Drug Store across the street from my current retail store. Wade would go to the store after hours and fill prescriptions and let me charge medicine if I was short on cash. I never had to worry about the wrong medicine getting into the bottle.

My how that industry has changed! Wade decided to leave the retail drug business and close his store, but I sure miss the way he did business. It used to be a pleasure to go to the drug store. Not only did you get your medicine, but you got to visit with your neighbors and friends, talk Tennessee football, and most importantly, receive Wade's signature smile and kind words. That drug store is like a lot of things–an era gone by, replaced with chain stores. Now there is nothing special about your prescription purchase. You just get it (if you can afford it) and go home. No relationships are formed, no sincere kind words are said, and there is no interest in your well-being.

I am saddened that my children and grandchildren may never experience service like that. If the local consumers had realized what an important jewel we had with independent drug stores, and not been lured in by the glamour of big chain stores, we could still be enjoying that type of business atmosphere today. What a shame. Wade never let anyone leave without their medicine, even if they didn't have the money to pay for it. Try that at the chain store. God bless Wade Wilson for the many years he gave to our Nashville business community.

Not too long ago I was at the doctor's office waiting to see the doc. Usually, when the exam is over, we visit for a little while. He usually asks how my business is going. We talk about the economy, and we share thoughts about the challenges that are the same in both our businesses. I did not share this with him, and maybe I will if it happens again, but I witnessed something while in the waiting room. Sometimes it's best to not say anything. Usually problems have a way of taking care of themselves. I saw a lady who worked for that facility come out of a door marked "Employees Only." When she came out she was telling the other lady in that room, "It's not my job." Now I don't have a clue what she was talking about. Whatever it was, I'm sure it wasn't her job, and she was probably right. It just looked unprofessional on her part, especially in that professional environment.

The next week I was honored to speak to the patient advocacy board at another hospital on the topics of customer service, compassion, kindness, and encouragement. After I spoke, the hospital's CEO walked with me to my car. As we were saying our goodbyes, he saw a piece of paper on the floor and picked it up, never breaking stride or his conversation with me. Of course I noticed. When I got back to my truck, I thought about the lady at the doctor's office. Picking up that piece of paper wasn't the CEO's job either.

See the difference? When I was addressing the hospital group that day, I told them about a doctor who works at a sister hospital. He is a cardiologist, recruited from a very prestigious teaching hospital out of town. They may not have known that, but I did. I was sent to him to let him run some tests on me and check out a problem. It turns out I'm ok. This doctor was something special. Not only had he distinguished himself in his field, his customer service skills were impeccable. The way he did business reminded me of an old time doctor. Respect and great customer service has always worked, and it always will. This doctor gets it. He and his staff will always have plenty of patients, and they will always be a valuable asset to their hospital. Many of the doctors I know slow down, listen, and want to give the best service they can. So does the hospital management.

You see, good customer service started at the top, and it is working its way down to the entire staff. LPNs become registered nurses, one step at a time. It may not always be their job, but they are doing what it takes to give good customer service, take care of the patients and go the extra mile. People who do this are going to be the most successful.

I read a book one time written by a famous TV show host and real estate guru. He told a story about a restaurant he liked to visit. The guru ordered a particular brand of soft drink, knowing that the restaurant didn't sell that brand. In a few moments the waiter returned with the brand the guru ordered. When the guru questioned where the drink came from, the waiter said he went next door to the market and bought it. He did this to give the man what he ordered. The guru thought about that for some time. A few weeks later he returned to that restaurant to offer the waiter a job. He learned that the waiter no longer worked there because he had resigned to open his own restaurant. Good service works. It doesn't matter if you are a waiter, a nurse, a doctor, a CEO, or a tire guy.

The next time you get the chance to do a little extra at work, go ahead. The next person you have an interaction with, smile a little more and try to be a little more helpful. Be consistent and it will become your habit. You will start treating your spouse a little better. You will be a little more patient with your kids. Life will come a little easier. It has taken me a lifetime to learn this secret.

OPPORTUNITIES AND JOY

I mentioned that my mother broke her hip in an earlier chapter. My sister Mitzie came to Nashville from Texas to stay with her during her recovery. Someone in the family was with her around the clock until she passed. We were all fortunate to have spent those last months with her. Her mind was good until the end, so we really enjoyed some great stories from our mother.

As I mentioned before, Mitzie married a boy in the military. She left home when I was pretty young and she lived all around the world. She always lived so far away that she never really got to see me grow up. She never knew too much about my career. I went by the hospital most mornings before work, then returned after work, and of course on the weekends. My other siblings did, too. We all worked pretty well together to take good care of our mom. The girls did most of the work. My brother and I just held her hand, made her laugh and that sort of thing. While mamma was sleeping, Mitzie and I talked a lot about our lives and brought each other up to speed. I told her some of my stories and about some of my clients and their exciting lives.

Looking back I think that tough time brought all us kids closer together. One Saturday afternoon, my sister Brenda stayed with mamma while Mitzie, Linda and I went to lunch. When we got in the elevator, we met a young man wearing a University of Alabama hat. I looked at that young fellow and told him, "Roll Tide." He smiled back at me and said, "Roll Tide!" The door opened and he got off. Mitzie asked if I liked Alabama. Of course I said yes. I went on to tell her that Coach Bryant's sister had been my client before she died.

At lunch I thought she and Linda would like to hear about the Bear's sister. I told them how I had first met her at the store. When she pulled up in her old Buick, I didn't have a clue who she was. When I greeted her, she told me she wanted to buy a set of tires for her up-coming trip to Tuscaloosa. She wanted to be safe on her trip. I didn't think she would otherwise put too many miles on her car, so I did not want to over sell her. I asked all the right questions, so I could make a good recommendation and help guide her with her tire purchase. I asked if she drove a lot each year, and of course she didn't, but this trip was going to be long for her, and she was concerned about the condition of her old tires. So we got her car in the shop and I ushered her into the customer waiting area. She told me the postal service was making a stamp in honor of her late brother. Not knowing her, I thought, "Wow! He must be pretty famous." Now sometimes I'm not the sharpest tool in the shed. She told me she was going to Tuscaloosa and I still didn't put it together. When she mentioned the stamp, I said to her, "Oh, who is your brother?" She replied, "Paul Bryant!" She was kind enough to bring me back one of those stamps. This was the start of a friendship that lasted until her passing. I will tell you a little more about her a little later.

So my sister Linda said, “Wow!” during lunch. Mitzie didn’t say anything. She just smiled and listened. The next morning I went to the hospital early so Mitzie could take a break and eat breakfast. When she returned, the TV was on and a commercial came on advertising old hit records that had been digitally re-mastered and put together as a collection. Two of the entertainers advertised were my friends and customers, but I didn't tell Mitzie that I knew them because I was afraid she wouldn’t believe me.

Shortly after that, mother was transferred to a rehab facility to continue her hip recovery. Mitzie had to return home for a few weeks. Before she left, she asked if I had ever seen a movie called "Secondhand Lions." I hadn’t. Mitzie told me it was about these two old brothers that wound up helping raise an orphaned nephew. They were full of these farfetched outlandish stories about their lives. My sister said my stories reminded her of those movie characters. Of course I had to rent it. What a great movie! After watching it I still don’t know if she believes all my stories or not. Maybe she was just processing them.

My job has allowed me to wait on some pretty interesting people. Politicians, singers, songwriters, musicians, Grammy winning producers, authors, coaches on all levels, athletes on all levels, brain surgeons, attorneys, judges, CEO’s of big companies, racecar drivers, waitresses, block layers, electricians, painters…you get the idea. I’ve met people in just about every vocation there is. Sometimes we are a little wowed by their work. If you are a client or have ever been to our store, you know there is a common denominator. We treat everyone the same. Most of the famous people don't act famous. They need to get their cars fixed, too. I have found that most famous people are interested in other people's lives, and they visit with other customers just like neighbors do. When someone famous gets in their car and leaves, sometimes I hear other customers saying, "That sure was a nice person. I have always heard that. I sure am glad I got to meet them."

My mother really liked Elvis. One of the prettiest songs Elvis ever did was a song titled "Always on my Mind." It wasn't a gospel song, but since it was one of my mother's favorites, we had it played at her funeral.

One of the co-writers is a client and friend named Wayne Carson. Wayne is such a funny guy. One day he brought enough fried chicken and sweet tea to feed Nolensville Road. We sat at the counter in the shop and ate chicken and told stories all afternoon. I am so honored to have such talented friends such as Wayne. Different customers stopped in that day, ate a chicken leg and told a story or two. I am thankful daily for the incredible job I have.

Wayne Carson and his wife Wyndi

It is easy to tell stories about famous people. I also like to share incredible stories about people who are not so famous but have done acts of kindness that need to be celebrated. All of these stories are neat to me. I may write another book since there are so many and it is hard to recall all of them at one time. I will share a few to whet your appetite. Some you may find them as great as I do.

One of the finest singers and guitar players ever was the Late Billy Grammer. Kim and I go to church with Mr. Grammer's daughter, Donna and her husband David. Some years ago Donna had a birthday party at her house for Mr. Grammer, and invited Kim, Bradley and me. We enjoyed picking, listening to Billy sing some of his hits and most of all hearing some of his stories. He told the story of when he, Mel Tillis, and Grandpa Jones decided to drive out west and play together acoustically at clubs at night and fish during the day. Mr. Grammer told of their adventures on the way. Mr. Grammer had an inherited eye disease and could not see very well. It eventually took his eyesight. Mel had a stuttering problem and it was difficult for him to talk, and Grandpa could not hear very well. They got lost and Mr. Grammer was navigating, trying to look at a map upside down that he couldn't see. Grandpa knew they were in trouble because Mel had a hard time asking for directions, and Grandpa couldn't hear the directions when they found someone to ask. Their entire trip was full of those types of scenarios and adventures.

Mr. Grammer owned a guitar factory and made custom guitars for many entertainers, and sold to the public. They were beautiful handmade instruments. He sold his business in the 1970s. Later the factory burned and the company never recovered. I am very fortunate to own one of his guitars. My friend Harold Weakley sold it to me in 1978. Harold wanted me to have it and sold it to me at a very reasonable price, or I could not have afforded it. Mr. Grammer played it that night at his birthday party. Bradley and I own many guitars, but my favorite three are the Grammer, a special Grand Ole Opry edition Martin that I bought from the late Bobby All, and a 1930 Vagabond that was my dad's. If you're going to live in Nashville, you must own a guitar and know at least three blue grass chords. Speaking of blue grass, the late Bill Monroe was my customer too!

Mr. Grammer was not only a singer and player; he was a great songwriter as well. Two of his great hits are "Traveling On" and "Cotton Fields." Harold Weakley told me about Mr. Grammer and his band traveling from one show to the next in the 1950s in a station wagon that was pulling a trailer. One of the band members was having marital problems. Mr. Grammer listened to the member's story for about 200 miles and then pulled an envelope and a pencil out of the glove box and wrote a song. He sold the song to Eddie Arnold for a sizable amount of money. Eddie Arnold had a hit record on that song.

Mr. Grammer is gone now, but has left a great legacy behind, and I sure am glad to have known him and called him my friend.

I'm glad to know and have as customers other music legends, such as Sonny James and Brenda Lee. What a delight each of them are to me. I love to hear their stories. Ronnie Shacklett, Brenda Lee's husband, has a great story of meeting Jackie Gleason on the set of "Smokey and the Bandit," one of the movies Brenda worked on. Each of these star entertainers are just like the folks next door, except they have a great God given talent.

There are many families that do business with us. We are so thankful for each one. One family I want to tell you about has done many acts of kindness. The man is a barber, his name is Harvey Barnes, and one year just before Christmas he came by the shop with his truck loaded down with bicycles. The back seat was crammed with presents. When I asked him about it, he said he bought the toys to give away to needy kids in his home town. Some years later I found out that his niece Sissy, gave one of her kidneys to a young girl she had met just because it was a match and the girl needed it. If that don't get your fire started your wood might be wet.

We go to church with Jack Oliver who played football with the Chicago Bears. What a gentle giant! I am proud to call him a friend. A few years ago we had a terrible flood in Nashville. The damage was in the millions and millions of dollars. Lives were lost, homes were lost; and many lives were changed forever. Many of our customers were impacted by the flood. The flood was kind of like the recession. People asked if the flood affected us, and the answer is not much directly, not even enough to mention, considering the devastation all around us. But it affected many of our customers, so yes it had an effect on us, too. When our customers are hurting, we hurt for them.

I had been in the hospital with pneumonia and just returned home. I couldn't actively help in the flood relief effort, but I could help financially, and I could be an encouragement to others that were physically helping. Of course I prayed for the victims and the relief workers. Fortunately, our employees were not affected much by the flood. Jack Oliver, my gentle giant friend from church, is also one of the staff pastors. He worked tirelessly to help flood victims. He helped put together teams to go out and tear out ruined sheetrock and remove trash and debris.

After a few days a national news team came to cover stories about the cleanup effort. Neighbors and total strangers bonded together to help each other through this tough time. There were two real famous singers, a husband and wife that the media interviewed alongside of my friend. Jack didn't know who they were, but they were all working side by side. Jack thought they were working on their home, but he was so busy he never really noticed who they were. They were Tim McGraw and Faith Hill—both famous, and both helping, too. I'm so proud of my friends that worked so hard for our community. I am very proud to live in a city that practices what so many preach.

Other friends like Richard Walton helped restore a flooded church, and David and Tammy Travis prepared hot meals for flooded neighborhoods for almost a year. God bless them. These are the difference makers.

It is good to have a job that allows me to interact with so many wonderful people. I must say that is the best part of my job.

I couldn't write a book and not tell you about an interesting fellow named Johnny Shealy. Charlie Watson, a longtime customer and friend, introduced me to Johnny. I let Johnny make payments so it was easier for him to afford his car maintenance expenses. We began a friendship that lasted as long as he lived. Johnny danced to a little different drum than most people. When you first meet Johnny, you might think he is a little slow, or maybe had a head injury at some time in his life. He may have had a mental challenge in some way, I don't really know. Johnny was much like the rain man. He could remember who played on the Grand Ole Opry, what they sang and what time they performed. He knew the birthday and birthplace of each Opry star. Johnny lived alone in an apartment about two miles from our retail store. His family lived in North Carolina. When we serviced his car, we drove him home. He always wanted to be home to watch "The Price is Right." Some years ago he wanted to be on the show, so he drove across the country to Hollywood. They didn't let Johnny on the show, but he got to be in the studio audience. If he had been a contestant, I bet he would have been the big winner. The motor blew on his car while he was on his trip. A church in downtown Nashville wired the money to help Johnny get his car going so he could get home. He made payments to that church for about ten years until he repaid every cent.

Sometimes Johnny ran out of money before he received his monthly social security check. He would come by the store to borrow some money to get him by for a few days. When he came in the door, he would say, "Hello, I'm Johnny Cashless." After that, he would say, "I need to go see the Colonel, and I will have your money on the first." By "the Colonel," he meant Kentucky Fried Chicken. His favorite places to eat were KFC, Taco Bell and Arby's. He always had coupons in his car. Those restaurants were usually close to exits along the interstates.

He planned another trip to see a high school classmate that lived in California. He went to California from Tennessee via Florida. When he returned home he told me about his trip and the damage his car sustained along the way. He kept a journal of expenses that he let me read. I noticed he stayed in Oklahoma about three days. I said, "Johnny, you must have liked that place."

"That's where my car sustained rear end damage in a traffic accident," he said. "There I was in Oklihoma, wanting a Cokiecola. I had a trunk full and could not get to it." You see the authorities impounded his car while they waited for his driver's license to arrive from Arizona. Johnny accidentally left it at a library.

Johnny liked to make sentences rhyme. Sometimes he would come into the store when I had several customers waiting, and say, "I need a Bassectomy." That meant he needed me to do some work on his car. It was always interesting to listen to him describe what was wrong with his car. On more than one occasion, he came in making a siren noise, "EEEER, Blue Boy done got me." That meant he had been stopped by the police with a tail light bulb out. It embarrassed me at first when ladies were present and he said that Bassectomy stuff, but as the years went by I learned more about Johnny. I realized that there were a few people that were really important to him and I was one of those people.

A few years ago Johnny was killed in a car crash out of state on one of his excursions. I think he went to sleep at the wheel. Sometimes, while changing a bulb in a customer's car, I will smile and think, "Blue Boy done got me." Johnny's simplicity, sincerity, loyalty and friendship meant a lot to me, and I sure am glad to have known him. Like so many of my old friends that are gone now, he left me with some great stories and fond memories.

Speaking of Blue Boy and the police department, Miss Kim has been stopped by the police several times in the last few months. The children and I have sure teased her about that.

Occasionally, I will get to do something that, if it weren't for my job, I would have never have been able to do. Of course with those adventures come some stories to tell. In an earlier chapter, I told you about our racing days and advertising with our logo on race cars, winning track championships, carrying our friends, family, customers and employees to the sky boxes to watch the races, and eat barbecue. Those were fun times. If it hadn't been for our business we would have never gotten to experience that.

About the same time, we rented the race track one afternoon to shoot a TV commercial. I stood in the middle of the track and the race car came screaming down the track, coming to a stop right behind me, so I could touch the car and deliver my lines. That was a fun commercial to do, however there were several problems. I kept jumping out of the way. I was afraid the car was going to hit me. Then the engine was so loud, it drowned out my voice. We finally got the driver to kill the engine and coast up behind me. After the shoot the driver took me for a couple of hot laps in the car.

Another time a vendor sent me to Bristol raceway to a driving school. I got to take a stock car ten laps around the track. I had a renewed respect for professional drivers. Those ten laps wore me out.

Another vendor let me go to the racetrack just outside Salt Lake City and drive some pretty fast cars for a couple of days.

At the proving grounds in Texas, I got to see the process of testing new tires and got to drive pretty erratically out there.

I have had the opportunity to attend dealer meetings through the years at some pretty nice places. I've been to Hawaii twice, Acapulco and Las Vegas. Getting to see the U.S. Arizona Memorial at Pearl Harbor was a terrific honor and a privilege. I got to send one of my kids to the Pro Bowl in Hawaii—all great trips because of my business.

The best thing about my job is the opportunity to earn a living for my family. Any retail business is confining. There isn't much time off; seventy hour work weeks are common. Running a business isn't for everyone, but it is all I know. I have never had a job that I was off Saturdays, but I have never opened on Sunday.

Our business has let us earn the income needed to educate our children. Both have finished college now. After Brad graduated college this year, Miss Kim and I were reminiscing, and we realized we had met our main goals for starting our business. So now it's time to set some NEW goals.

I have also had the opportunity and honor to be the master of ceremonies at a client's 50th wedding anniversary and at a fundraiser for a radio ministry. I've spoken to several groups and appeared on a local TV show. All of which would have never been possible if I hadn't owned my own business. I wouldn't have written this book either. I have had the opportunity to sell tires to two former Governors, one deputy governor, two county Sheriffs, numerous judges, politicians, entertainers, and I don't know how many ex-convicts.

FAMILY LIFE

As I write this and prepare to talk a little about our family life, two of the greatest events of our families' existence have occurred: the birth of our granddaughter, Langley Grace Bass. I told our boys that they are special, just not as special as those grandbabies. My great grandfather, Thomas Langley, served in the Civil War. My grandmother was Mattie Langley and my father was named T.L. after his grandfather. My brother was named Thomas Langley. Langley is a pretty special name in our household.

Langley and Luke dressed up in their Alabama football gear

The other greatest event in our family is the birth of our grandson Luke. The name Luke was chosen from the great author of the third gospel of the New Testament. Luke is such a fine name for such a blessing from heaven. I'm kind of like Forrest Gump—they are the most beautiful things I have ever seen.

You have probably heard the old saying, "Behind every good man is a good woman." I agree. A few times in the book I have referred to my darling wife as Miss Kim. I also call her Buddy sometimes. In 1989 cell phones were new, and we had a service truck that I will tell you about in a little while. Instead of radio dispatch we used a cell phone. I was on a service call and had someone in the truck with me. The phone rang and it was Miss Kim. When we had just about wrapped up our phone conversation, I said, "Alright Buddy. Love you. See you in a little while." My passenger asked who was on the phone. I told him it was my wife, and he asked

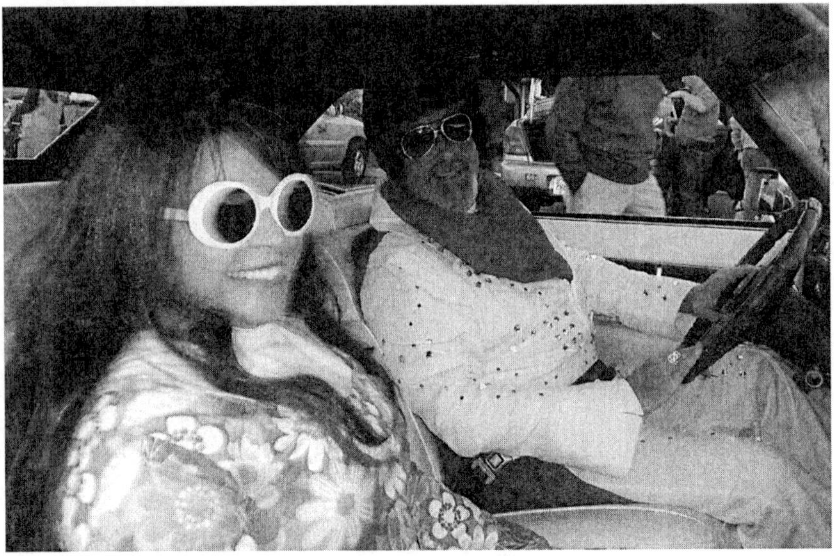

Miss Kim and I dressed as Priscilla and Elvis at our church's Trunk-or-Treat

why I called her Buddy. I replied that she is my buddy. Kim used to teach Sunday school to six and seven year old kids. They all called her Miss Kim, so I started calling her that around the kids at church and the name stuck.

If success is going to happen during the challenging work day, you need a good home life to come home to at the end of the day. There are always going to be ups and downs, and challenges to deal with, but it's important to have a supportive wife and family if you are a business person.

Miss Kim and I are partners in business, marriage, finances, children, household, good times and bad. We are in it together. Sometimes she has to come to the store and work, but her office is at home, right next to the kitchen. She takes care of the paper flow, receivables, and that sort of thing. If a customer needs a copy of an invoice, or we need an account balance, we give her a call, an email or a text. With her office at home she can manage running the household and the jobs she needs to do for the company. We started that way when we first went into business and the children were little. Quite frankly, I don't know how she gets it all done.

I take care of day to day operations with the help of my staff at the store. Miss Kim takes care of the house and its operations. I will not rock the boat unless she asks me to. When I come home, supper is ready, the house is always clean, it's warm in the winter and decorated for Christmas. She has worked hard and continues tirelessly to see that the children and I have everything we need. If there is anything I need to deal with or need to know before I hit the driveway, she always lets me know. We never have fussed much. We both have worked pretty hard to avoid fussing. If you are happy at home, usually you are happy at work. The old song says, "If you're happy and you know it then your face will surely show it."

When Kim and I first got married, we didn't have much in the way of material things and certainly not much money. My mother and dad received blocks of government cheese each month. They could not eat it all and shared with us. We ate grilled cheese, cheese and crackers, nachos, macaroni and cheese, and pimento cheese. I ate so much pimento cheese the first two years we were married, I didn't start eating it again until last year. When Charlie was a little boy, we went to Florida for our vacation and we packed a picnic lunch of tuna fish and pimento cheese to conserve our money. We could not afford to eat out and travel, too. We stopped along the way and ate our picnic lunch at the tables at the rest stops. Recently, I needed to go to Bowling Green, Kentucky to get a wheel for a customer. I asked Kim to go with me. We took a picnic lunch. It reminded us about our travels with the kids. I think the struggles early on, when we didn't have anything but each other and the kids, helped make our life so good now. We had to depend on one another so much back then it has become our way of life.

Looking back, I think it was a good thing that we did struggle some. Our oldest son Charlie and our daughter-in-law Amy live across the country in Utah. Charlie has to travel four states with his job. He is gone a lot, and as I am writing this book, Amy and Langley are home alone much of the time. I'm sure it is hard on them now, but it will probably make their life and marriage stronger in the years to come.

Each generation seems to have their struggles and hardships. In the 1960s when I was growing up, I can remember traveling from Dickson, Tennessee to nearby Waverly, We often stopped at a carry-out Barbecue joint to buy some sandwiches. Then we stopped along highway 70 W at the road side picnic table to eat on the way to my grandparent's house. I wonder if families still do that, or if they stop at fast food restaurants.

Amy, Luke, Langley, Charlie and Biscuit posing for their Christmas card

Each stage of the children's life growing up was a lot of fun. It is fun to watch them now as young adults starting their own career paths.

Our home life would have been mundane to a lot of people, but it suited us fine. We worked and came home, helped with homework, watched a little TV, and did it all again the next day. Miss Kim made sure home life was good. You sure can't ask for much more than that.

Without a stable home life, your business life will struggle. I never had to travel in my career. I went to the store, did my work and came home. A lot of people have to travel to make a living. I enjoyed getting away the few times I had to travel for meetings, but it was always good to get home.

Me and Miss Kim with Charlie and Amy at their wedding in Florida

We are not quite empty nesters just yet. Our oldest son Charlie is married and lives in the western United States, where he is a sales representative for Michelin of North America. Bradley has recently graduated college and is a recording engineer. He still lives at home. We are very proud of both our boys. When folks brag on them, my chest swells some, then I have to tell them their mother did a good job raising them.

Charlie, Miss Kim and myself with Bradley after his graduation from MTSU

I addressed a group of professionals just after Brad graduated college with honors. I told those ladies and gentlemen about Brad graduating magna cum laude—and all these years I thought he got his intelligence from me. However after graduation, I overheard Miss Kim tell one of my sisters Brad's accomplishments were due to the nurturing of his mother. The group said they should have asked my wife to speak instead of me. Well, I guess so!

I have an old friend I want to include in the family section because he is pretty close to family. We feel like most of our dear friends are family, but we can't mention them all in a short period of time.

We call this friend Bama Jim. He is the biggest Alabama fan of all time. A local sports announcer gave him the name Bama Jim, many years ago. Bama is very well read, loves Bama football, and is arguably one of the funniest guys I have ever been around. After my dad passed away, I sought advice from Bama from time to time. He always had time for me. He took me and my

Bama Jim Johnson and his wife Eulene

boys to some Bama games with his grandson. What good times. Bama retired early in life and helped me out at the store, so we spent a lot of time together and naturally became very close.

One time, Bama compared me and my life to the movie character George Bailey, from "It's A Wonderful

Life." George was a business man who didn't have a lot of money but was the richest guy in town. I love that movie, and I think that was the highest compliment I ever received.

Miss Kim and myself at a Bama game in Tuscaloosa

Shredder, Brad, me and Charlie watching a Bama game from home

Wealth can be measured in many ways. Much like George Bailey, I may not have a very big bank account, but I have riches beyond measure. My family and friends have made my life the best.

When I was young and starting out at the Nolensville Road store, the president of Universal addressed us at a manager's meeting during a time of slight economic challenges. He told the group that if he lost all the money he had but could keep his family, friends, and good staff, he could earn it all back pretty fast. I think he was driving home the importance of having a strong appreciation for family. I believe that with all my heart.

Kim made sure we did all we could as a family to instill that strong foundation in our kids.

I told you earlier in this chapter I would tell you more about our service truck. There was an old business man on Nolensville Road that was an icon for many years. I applied for a job with his company in 1977. When he finally called to offer me a job, I had already gone to work with another company. When he retired in the late eighties, he came to see me. I had only met him a few times, but he had watched my career. He came to talk to me about giving me some of his commercial accounts, no strings attached. He told me how he had been servicing them and about the pricing structure he developed for them. He said the only thing I would have to do is buy a service truck and hire a man to run it. Sounded simple enough, so we did it. The extra business generated up to $250,000 annually in revenue, but a whole share of problems went with it. We operated that part of the business from 1988-1997. The last couple of years it just broke even and we shut it down in 1997. It had its worries, but it was kind of fun for a while.

We had some truck accounts, tree trimming company accounts, some contractors, and we averaged about eight calls a day. One of the problems was if the serviceman was out, I had to run the truck, or if we got behind, we had to work at night.

Kim didn't like me on the work truck at night alone. She was afraid I would get hurt and have no way to get help. So sometimes she went with me. One time I had to go fix a flat on a dump truck at a cemetery. It got dark and I wasn't finished and couldn't see. Miss Kim told me to hurry up because it was spooky in the back of that cemetery. I told her the dead ones would not bother her. But I did hurry up; it was spooky.

Another time we did a job out of town. We took the kids, like it was a road trip. Kim and the boys stayed at the motel, I did the job, got back, we went to eat, shopped a little, and drove home. Closing that division was a good move, but it did leave us with some fond stories. Bradley was just a baby when we first got the service truck business. The tree trimming company had a guy that was in charge of their trucks, and he had our home phone number so he could call before the store opened to schedule any repairs, so his trucks could be first on our docket for the day. But his calls kept waking up Bradley. Kim would answer the phone, and he would say in a loud voice, "I need a tire man and I need him bad." About the third time in the first week, Miss Kim told him the tire man was in the shower, and if he woke up the baby again, he was going to get the tire man's wife instead.

In closing this chapter, family is what motivates me to work hard.

ADVERTISING AND MARKETING

There are so many ways to advertise. When I'm asked what works best for our business, I tell folks, "Word of mouth." That is the most effective form of advertising we have found: friends, telling friends, family telling family, neighbors telling neighbors, employees telling their friends and family.

It is important to get your name out. In the early years, we used a lot of print advertising. Back in the 70s when I first came to town to work, the newspaper was the best place for tire ads. The company I worked for placed full page ads in the sports section every Sunday. We did some TV and radio commercials, billboards and fence billboards at ball fields. Of course, we had several stores and vast co-op advertising funds available to us. It paid off. Each advertising segment complimented the other.

I remember hearing a slogan I'll share with you. "Early to bed, early to rise, work like heck, and advertise." I cleaned one part up.

When we started Bass Tire, we wasted a lot of money at first by shooting in the dark and hitting nothing. We met a salesman at a local radio station who helped write a script, and we ran a few radio spots. One of my cousins is in the office equipment business. Radio works well for his industry, but it didn't seem to hit our target of customers. Maybe we did not run on enough stations, or maybe we didn't run them long enough. We had a limited ad budget and we needed to find our niche, so we hired an ad agency.

Joe, our ad representative, was an older well-spoken gentleman. Because of the success of my previous company, he thought we would try newspaper. Joe's earlier career was in newspaper, and there was no one that knew that media better than he did. We ran eighth page ads in the showcase section of the Sunday paper once each month. We had better results with newspaper than we did with radio, but we still weren't hitting home runs. Then Joe mentioned cable TV. We could afford to try TV and measure our results. We bought some cable ad packages and became one of Nashville's cable TV regulars. It really helped our business take off.

However, even with our co-op dollars we were spending most of our profits on TV advertising. Combined with our race car sponsorships, previous newspaper ads, and current TV our logo and name recognition began to climb. People were talking about our ads and referrals started coming in. We were finally starting to see the return on our money.

We staggered our packages so it appeared that we were on TV more than we really were. We tried different types of ads to generate interest with our customers. We shot commercials to run during stock car races. We shot golf ads to appeal to the golfers. We had a peewee football team participate in a shoot during football season. We used customers in ads for testimonials. For the next few years, I was on TV as much as the weather man—or least it seemed that way. Once we got our business built up, we decided to back off. Instead of new ads every eight weeks, we ran only three campaigns a year. We increased the number of ads bought per campaign, but reduced the number of campaigns.

We always ran a commercial at Christmas, not only to attract new business, but also to thank everyone for their business and wish them a Merry Christmas. We started running a spring commercial and one during college basketball finals. Those three TV campaigns continue to work the best for us.

As the years have gone by, my hair has gone gray and I have put on a few pounds. I just don't look as good on TV as I used to. If I were on TV now as often as I used to be I might run off more people than I brought in! Aaron is our spokesperson now. Aaron is my young understudy. He's been with our company since he graduated high school. He started out in the shop and has worked his way to management. Aaron appeals to the younger crowd as well as our existing older customers. Our Christmas commercial usually starts out with Aaron introducing himself and our company, thanking everyone for their business and wishing them a Merry Christmas. Then he calls on Santa Claus to tell everyone about our Christmas specials. Then I step into frame wearing a Santa costume, saying, "HO! HO! HO!" We did that format for a couple of years, and then tried a fireside commercial by a Christmas tree without Aaron or Santa. Everyone wanted Aaron and Santa. So the Santa ads came back and they still remain today. So many of our customers are older and don't get out as much as they used to. They really look forward to seeing those Santa ads. Santa Claus appeals to young and old.

Aaron and myself appearing in one of our Christmas commercials

Me, Luke, Biscuit and Langley shooting our latest Christmas commercial

The last few years our spring ads feature me and Aaron sitting in chairs in my office in front of my desk like we're having a casual chat. We just happen to be plugging a particular tire, no pun intended. When we are at church or at a restaurant, folks will come by and say, "Hey, I saw you guys on TV." Now we can also reach our customers using Facebook. I would have never dreamed of that type of media when we started in business.

In the old days with Universal Tire we did some live commercials on a popular morning TV show, "The Ralph Emery Show." That was very effective as well. The show had a very loyal following, and some of my older customers still remember those days. Many of the businesses that advertised on that show are still in business today. Most of the band members were local session players and many played at the Opry. Many of the musicians, one of the weathermen and co-host, Dan McDaniel, are still our customers today. That was a fun way to advertise. John Morgan and I would do the weekly spots on The Ralph Emery Show. One of the guys on the show was Lightning Chance. He was a bass player. He sat in on our ads many times, and made them go really smooth for us. He was a natural. He was in the movie, "Coal Miner's Daughter." What a funny guy.

We shot a Thanksgiving ad one year at a customer's house. Toney Catignani's family is very special to me. It is a large family and mealtime reminds me of the Walton's on TV, except my friend's family is much bigger. My friend's parents' home had a very large den. Most Sundays they moved the furniture along the walls and set up huge tables, and the entire family ate together. They moved their Thanksgiving dinner up a couple of weeks so we could film a TV commercial in their home at their table. It sure was something. All that food and all that family—we were all together and giving thanks at the holiday season, and thanking our customers, too. The Catignani family has allowed me to be a part of their extended family, for all these years. I can't tell you the warmth, kindness and love Toney's family has shown Kim, the boys and me. I love the Catignani's for many reasons, but their emphasis on family, service to God and love for each other and their friends, is what makes them the real deal and so special to me.

ACTS OF KINDNESS

In a previous chapter, I told you about the lady that gave one of her kidneys to someone in need. I told you about her uncle giving the under privileged children in his home town a good Christmas. I would like to share a few more stories of kindness in this chapter as they come to mind.

There are so many it is hard to remember them all. I told you about the flood and how a church pastor worked so hard to make a difference. I have taken hundreds of calls through the years from clients concerning family members, friends, church members and even strangers in need, where my clients said, "Give them what they need, and I will come by and pay you." This chapter is dedicated to those acts of kindness. Why do people do that?

Well I'm not a psychologist, but I have my thoughts. I think there are several reasons. The biggest: it's right thing to do. Some people have such a big heart and are always looking for ways to bless other people. I think a lot of people realize that the Lord has blessed them beyond measure and little acts of kindness are a way of giving back. I think the Lord lays acts of kindness on our hearts. Maybe folks remember when they were younger and in need and someone stepped up to the plate.

I'm a Shriner and the Shrine Hospitals for children is one of my favorite charities. We offer no charge treatment for orthopedic and burn patients.

There is an upscale shopping area in Nashville, and I often work a Shriner's paper sale there to raise funds for our hospitals. Two years in a row the same lady put a sizable check in my bucket. I noticed she walked with a limp. The second time I met her she told me that when she was a little girl she was operated on at Shrine hospital to help her walk. She had more surgery as she grew up, but she was so appreciative, she wanted to give back.

I have a late friend that was a contractor. His family business was one of the oldest and largest construction companies in the U.S. He, too, was a Shriner. I saw him that very day I met the other lady. He told me that his company was building one of the hospitals. He went $250,000 over budget and never billed the Shriners for the over run.

Each year the Shrine circus comes to town, and I give away general admission tickets at the store to children who come in with their parents. We have a commercial account that takes care of mentally handicapped adults. When these adults get to come to our store, they feel like they are on a field trip. I see the same clients when they visit our store for service on their van. They are grown but have a child's mentality. One of the young ladies came to the counter to speak to me and saw the clown picture on the circus ticket. She asked what it was. I told her and asked if she had ever been to the circus. She had not. I told their caretaker that if she would take their clients to the circus, I would arrange for as many tickets as she would use. That was such a blessing to me that I've also sent them to our local baseball stadium to see some games.

The same year we got to send some folks to the circus, I was asked to do a project for the Make a Wish Foundation. The National Football League sent me a truck load of display footballs to inflate so players could autograph them to give away at a local Make a Wish dinner. As we handled those balls I couldn't help but think of the children and their families that would be touched by getting a signed ball. All it cost me was air. A little hot air and some circus tickets were a highlight of my year. On the surface it seems pretty insignificant, but after some thought I realized what a blessing I received.

It didn't take too many years for the news to get out about free circus tickets at Bass Tire. One Saturday just about noon, our closing time, a young man from the neighborhood came by to see if we had any circus tickets left. I only had one, but he needed one for himself, his wife and their two children. So I gave him some money to buy the additional tickets at the door. Aaron called the young man over and gave him some more money and told him to buy popcorn and soft drinks for his family when he got to the circus. Aaron looked at me after the young fellow left, and said, "You didn't think I was going to let you get all the blessing, did you?"

Well, that is what I want to see. Some customers have seen a little of what we have done with the circus and many have sent checks to cover the cost of the children's tickets. This is just a glimpse of the great people I get to wait on and work with every day.

One morning, a sergeant on the police department was waiting when we opened. With him was a young woman with an infant and the spare tire on her car. He or one of his officers was on patrol and saw the young woman in need. When they heard her story, they pooled some money together to get her a room for the night, a meal, baby formula, diapers and traveling money. They changed her flat and brought her to me to get it repaired so she could get back on the road. The police sergeant told me some of her story and said to do what she needed and he would pay her bill. Well, I couldn't let the officers get all the blessing. She reached her destination and wrote me a letter of thanks. Her sincere gratitude and letter really touched my heart. The content of her letter could have brought a tear to a glass eye.

A young man that ran our service truck got his eye put out when he was a little boy. Dr. Sloan was an eye doctor whose practice was down the street. He has gone on to be with the Lord now, but his wife still comes in. The doctor was a kind and well-loved part of our Nolensville Road business community. He met my employee and asked me how he lost his eye. The doctor told me he could have an eye painted to match his good eye and attach the muscles to it so it would turn and no one could tell he had a glass eye. Of course this would enhance his appearance. There's no telling what that would have cost, but you know how much was billed. No charge!

I told you a little bit about the flood we had in Nashville in 2010. A neurosurgeon does business with us, and I heard he did his first brain surgery at age 29. That sounds about right, knowing how smart he is. He told me the story of a lady he met whose car got caught in the flood while she was trying to evacuate some homeless people. The surgeon said the lady had been a corporate attorney in Atlanta and had been called to preach. She left her old life to minister to the homeless in Nashville. The doctor wanted me to evaluate the repair needs on her car and send him the bill. I told the doctor that anything was possible, but not always feasible. That was the case with that lady's car. She needed a car. He asked me to find her a good used car. You can guess how that turned out. One used SUV, no charge.

You see, having a good job and a great lifestyle loses its luster if you can't give back. We all have the ability to give back. It is not always with our finances; however if we can, we need to put our money where our mouth is, otherwise, it's just lip service.

Success in business is not always measured by the size of the bank account. Kindness, encouragement, giving, hope...all the important virtues of life, are learned one step at a time. All the people mentioned in this chapter learned these virtues. I've learned much from them. Some of the greatest lessons in my book have nothing to do with selling tires. Or maybe they have everything to do with selling tires, or whatever it is that you do. I hope this paragraph makes sense. I think it's one of the most important paragraphs in the book.

Some of the greatest lessons in my book have nothing to do with selling tires. Or maybe they have everything to do with selling tires.

There are so many more stories to share, but I think you get the picture. They are different but yet the same: people helping people.

Sunday the preacher told about a lady he could have helped on a recent trip, but before he realized there was a need, it was over. He missed an opportunity to help someone. It bothered him enough to pray over it. He asked the Lord to open his eyes for opportunity to make a difference, big or small.

I thought about that while having lunch with my wife earlier in the week. We went to a great hamburger restaurant in Nashville and had gotten our food. I saw a young girl in a wheelchair ordering her meal. Our little table was along the wall, and patrons had to come by our table to pay and get their food. I saw Miss Kim reach for her purse to give the girl some money. Kim did not know if the girl had the money for her meal but told the girl she knew how hard it was to find money in a backpack, and she wanted to buy her meal. It was over before I knew what was happening, but my sweetie saw the opportunity to show kindness, and I couldn't help but think about this incident during the sermon.

THE GREATEST SALESMAN EVER

In my career I've seen many great salesmen. I would like to tell you about a few of them and some of the things I learned from them. Aaron and I might be the best salesmen ever, but we were inspired by a few great men I'm going to tell you about.

Textbook salesmen warmly greet potential customers and introduce themselves. They remember the customer's name. They listen well to determine the customer's needs or wants, and they figure out which products fit the customer's needs best. They lead the customer. If the customer does not ask first, a good salesman will ask for the sale, close and collect. It's pretty simple. The salesman that is the best at delivering these things should be successful.

A little polish, but not too shiny.

A little bull, but don't stink.

Product knowledge, but don't overwhelm.

Always say thank you, and mean it.

If you don't know, say so.

Be yourself.

Always be a Professional.

Here are a few men whose methods impress me.

My old boss, John Morgan

My retired life insurance agent, John Carswell

My preacher, Gene Mims

An alarm component salesman, the late Butch Work

A food broker, whose biggest single sale was manure, Larry King

We are all salesman. Our employees are good salesmen. Their friends, family and neighbors are also salesmen. So are our children and spouses. But our company's best salesmen are our customers.

But our company's best salesmen are our customers.

We talked in an earlier chapter about how important word of mouth advertising is. When our friends and customers refer clients, they have already sold us and our business. All we have to do is take care of them.

My friend Larry King made one of his biggest sales on his blue tooth phone while fishing with his friend Tommy Cox. He called Tommy "Big Daddy." He told Big Daddy about his big sale and Big Daddy told him he should fish more. When Mr. Cox passed on to be with the Lord, Larry reminisced about that day. Everyone loved Big Daddy. I'll never forget Larry's words about his friend. "If Big Daddy liked you he would give you the shirt off his back. If he didn't he would go buy you one." No finer compliment could be paid. I'm proud to have known Tommy, and I'm proud to call Larry King my friend.

We all sell ourselves every day. I am constantly reinventing what we do in our business. By that I mean we change our menu, so to speak. We cook with the same ingredients, but we cook to order. Each of us is unique. Each customer may have to be waited on a little differently, but each is still waited on with the same care, kindness and respect.

Larry King and myself having lunch on one of our Harley rides

Giving good customer service never changes. The way you administer that service may change, but the old fashioned concept is the same.

If you are eating at a steak restaurant, the waiter may ask you how you like your steak cooked. Some people like their steak cooked medium, some like it well done. If they are all cooked well done, some people will not be happy. Aaron and I like to be good waiters and ask how our customers like their steak. Once we know, we try our best to have our cooks prepare the best steak the customer has ever tasted every time.

I like to use analogies, because we all can relate to them.

When asked how he is doing, my friend John Carswell, my retired insurance agent, will say, "This is the best day of my life until tomorrow." We attended a sales conference together one time and one of the speakers used that saying.

Often I answer the question of how am I doing, by saying, "Just right." I'm not fair, I'm not just okay, and I'm not even fine, I'm just right.

My friend Tim Hargrove from the police department loves that answer, so does Mel Overton, as his Dad used to say that. Sometimes I'll say, "I'm hanging in there like a hair in a biscuit." Sometimes the ladies will answer, "Oh, Steve!"

Sometimes I will say, "I'm better than I deserve." Now that usually inspires some conversation. Some will say that I have been listening to Dave Ramsey on the radio, that he says that. I'll answer, "Yep." Or sometimes I'll answer, "Where do you think he got it?"

I'll share with you a few tips that I try to work on each day to make me a better salesman and better business man.

Look good. I don't have that much to work with but appearance is important. Look sharp, think sharp.

I had a friend that worked for the first big corporate office machine company in the world. He fixed their brand of typewriters. That company's policy at the time was to wear a three-piece suit every day. As times changed, the typewriter left the work place, as did three-piece suits for their technicians. Logo branded golf shirts or logo branded dress shirts are the norm now.

One of my children is a sales rep for four western states. He calls on businesses like mine. His business dress attire is the logo branded shirts with kaki or dress slacks. Now his company used to require ties, but they changed their policy. They did not want their sales people to make their customers feel less professional than they were. Most companies tailor their dress code to fit their customers.

I have a friend and client in the clothing business. He calls himself the clothier to the stars. He always dresses like a million bucks. When I comment on how sharp he looks, he will reply, "That's my business."

I have another client that is a funeral director. When he is working, he wears a coat and tie.

When I'm at work, I wear a logo shirt. At church, I wear dress or casual dress attire, usually, a tie or sometimes coat and tie. With either, I try my best to look sharp and think sharp.

Having a good attitude is a key to sales success. No one likes negativity. Another one of my customers is a preacher. He asked to borrow some old batteries for props for a sermon about positives and negatives. I always try to be positive. When you can, turn a negative into a positive. One time Aaron sold a lady a set of tires. I saw her and spoke but did not know her. She was a new customer and we had not developed a relationship yet.

A few weeks after the visit for her tires, she returned to see me and was not happy. I was very busy. Aaron and Stan both tried to help her with no avail. I acknowledged her but she had to wait a few minutes before I could get to her. When I got off the phone and came out to greet her, she let me have it. She was upset because she had lost a hubcap. I apologized to her and assured her we would replace it. She continued to thrash me pretty hard and pointed out that her other hubcaps were installed incorrectly. I looked and she was right, the valve stems were not quite lined up with the space in the hubcap for them. I again agreed with her and assured her of resolution. I retrieved the VIN from her car so I could order her a new hubcap. I asked for her name and number, so I could call her when it came in. Well round three occurred. She informed me she wasn't going anywhere until the matter was resolved. I agreed to send a driver and get the hubcap from the dealer warehouse here in Nashville. Nothing I did was quite good enough for her. I knew she was a kind person and really didn't mean any animosity toward me. I needed to find some common ground, so we could connect and communicate a little better. I asked her where she attended church. She didn't tell me but she did ask me where I went. When I told her, she said one of her good friends also attended my church. I told the lady I knew her friend well, and I had given her friend a ride to Sunday school the previous Sunday on the church golf cart.

Now she began to feel a little more at ease. She was seated in the customer waiting area where she was comforted by another customer, a young girl, who assured her that we would take care of her problems. She became a little more settled until my driver got back from the dealer and we discovered he had the wrong cap. That is when she told me that the reason she was so upset. She wanted to go to the movie that day and was going to miss the matinee. Well, when my employee got back with the right hubcap, I escorted the nice lady to her car and received her blessings that everything was okay. I reached in my pocket and gave her twenty dollars for a movie ticket. She smiled and said it only cost ten, and I told her a girl needed popcorn with her movie. She hugged my neck and was on her way.

The next day she pulled up at the shop, and I thought, "Oh no!" She opened the back door of her car and asked if I liked bundt cake. Over the years she has brought many cakes to the shop. We have formed a true friendship all because I learned about turning a negative to a positive from a preacher who wanted to borrow a few batteries. I knew she was a kind and good person. I was taught a good lesson about patience, and getting kindness by first giving it.

When speaking to groups, I always mention kindness and how important it should be in life as well as in business. No matter your status in life, showing you care and being kind doesn’t cost much and pays off big dividends.

There is a story I like to tell about the kindness of an entertainer. When I was eleven years old in 1969, my mother and I went with our next door neighbor, Mrs. Work and her daughter, Kathy to Memphis to visit my uncle in the VA hospital there. Our old car probably would not make the trip from Dickson to Memphis, but our neighbor had a new car and thought it would be a nice day trip. We set out on our journey. After seeing my uncle we went to a barbecue joint for lunch, and lo and behold we were across the street from a mansion. In 1969 the biggest entertainer in the world lived in Memphis and we were eating lunch across the street from his house. After lunch we walked over to get a glimpse of the mansion. There was another lady looking as well, and she said if Elvis was home and if enough people were at his gate at dusk, he would ride a golf cart down the drive, stand on a stump, open the gates and everyone could go in and meet him and get an autograph. I asked my mother if we could stay. Sure enough, about 50-75 fans were waiting at dusk and the golf cart came down the drive. The gates opened and we all filed in. Being at the front of the gate, we were close to Elvis. He shook hands, answered questions, gave autographs, and was in no hurry. Even as a little kid, I can remember the kindness he showed to everyone.

One of our customers was a Nashville police officer named Calvin Hunter. Elvis was recording in Nashville in the 1950s and wanted two uniformed police officers to guard the studio while He was there. My friend Calvin got the assignment. The sessions were done at night over three days. Elvis bought dinner for everyone each night. At the end of the sessions, his staff was unsure what to pay the policemen. Elvis said to pay them what everyone else on the session made. Calvin thanked Elvis, and told him it was much more than he expected. He told Elvis that thanks to him his children would have a nice Christmas. That must have touched Elvis. Elvis produced a note pad and wrote down Calvin's name and address. He asked Calvin if he would like to work for him again and the ages of his children. Calvin worked for Elvis on two more occasions. For the next few years Calvin received a Christmas card from Elvis with a check for the same amount Calvin had been paid before and a hand written note from the super star. It read, "Hope your kids have a good Christmas. Love, Elvis." Calvin sure was proud and blessed because of his time with Elvis. After Calvin shared his story with me, I couldn't help but wonder just how many others Elvis blessed around the world? I am overwhelmed by that kind of generosity and kindness.

I had a customer who made a fortune in the cassette and CD business. He had a sea going vessel, a big boat. My friend knew I followed stock car racing. He told me stories about a famous driver that docked his boat next to his at Daytona. My friend said the boats were very similar, but his was bigger than the race car driver's boat. They formed a friendship through the years. I think it was he who told me that on Mondays after a Sunday race, the famous driver would get in his old pickup truck and drive around the North Carolina countryside. The driver often noticed the preacher of a small country church shoveling gravel back into the parking lot after a heavy rain. One day he stopped to talk to the preacher. Of course the preacher recognized the driver. The race car driver inquired about the gravel and drainage problems, and told the preacher he would have a paving crew come out and pave the lot to solve that problem at no charge to the church, but if he ever told where the money for the parking lot came from, he would have it all dug back up! A few years later that driver was killed in a car crash at Daytona. His name was Dale Earnhardt.

HARD WORK PAYS OFF

This is an important part of this book. Every successful person I have ever known has worked hard. On the outside to others, it may look like they have it easy, but that is seldom the case. Great athletes are born with a God given talent. But that's just the beginning; what follows is many hours of practice, body conditioning, proper diets—all the things it takes to be superb on game day. The great ones make it look so easy. They made the sacrifices and paid the price.

Great musicians really impress me as well. Like great athletes, they too are born with a God given talent. But they add countless hours of practice, learning all the aspects of their craft, and dealing with other big egos. After all that, the great ones make it look so easy.

Great business leaders are no different. They are good managers; they make goals and help their staff members make their own goals. Then they hit their projections. They are achievers. They are profitable. They are good with people, both employees and customers. Great business leaders repeat, year after year, and constantly challenge their staff to achieve their potential. Great professionals don't make excuses, they figure out great solutions. Business changes. As challenges present themselves, a great leader gets his team together and develops a winning game plan. They work together to rise above any stumbling block.

When I was young I tried to join the military. My blood pressure was too high and I was sent home on a bus. I became friends with two brothers who had met with a recruiter from the Army. They inspired me to join the military, too. The two brothers enlisted, and I never heard from them again. After I was grown I always thought I would have made a good Admiral in the Navy. I am pretty good at getting things done. With the right bunch of sailors and marines, we could get our supplies and men from point A to point B, defeat the enemy and get home.

Even though I never could serve our great nation in the military, I have had the honor and privilege to serve many of the men and women in our military. God bless them one and all. My brother was an Army Ranger, my father served in the south pacific theater in World War II. Our active and retired service men and women and the ones that made the ultimate sacrifice are all heroes to me. Their hard work and sacrifices are the reasons we can enjoy the freedoms and all the good our great country can afford us all. We all must always remember the hard work of our military personnel. I would like to share a few examples of how hard work paid off for some military friends and for America.

Today after church, I took Aaron and his family, Miss Kim and Brad out for lunch. Since we went to a popular eating place near our store, we knew many of the restaurant's customers. It took a while to make it to our table, since we stopped to visit. I really enjoy and look forward to this when we go out. Today we were seated next to a very special friend and his wife and daughter. It was an honor to ask the waitress to let me have their lunch ticket. You see Mr. Lee is not only a customer, he has referred business to us from his church and his family and we've been friends for 35 years. Mr. Lee is a former Marine. I noticed a lapel pin on his suit coat made in the shape of the famous picture of the Marines raising the flag on the battle of Iwo Jima. Mr. Lee isn't just any Marine with that pin; he was there! When the flag was raised the battle was still raging. When I complimented his lapel pin, his old eyes teared up. God bless that hero!

In 1985 Miss Kim and I bought a house on a pretty major thoroughfare in Nashville, Edmondson Pike, where we lived for about 16 years. We had been there for a few days and met our neighbors. Jimmy, one of the neighbors, and I became very good friends until his death a few years ago. Jimmy was a Vietnam veteran. He never talked much about his military service, but after we became very good friends, he told me a little bit about his service in Vietnam. He had been a sergeant in the Army. He served three tours in the Special Forces. To endure the hardships and horrors of war and to make it home came at a high price for my friend.

Just a few years before Jimmy died he came by the shop and asked if I had any cash. I said, "Sure, how much you need?" He said about a fifty dollar donation would do. I asked, "What project are you working on? Is that enough?" He had bought a red wagon to load down with fruit to pull through the halls of our VA hospital here in Nashville to bring a little Christmas cheer to some of the patients. God bless that hero. He continued to give back to our country and our vets until he died. It was an honor to be a pall bearer at his funeral. The preacher at his funeral is also one of my clients and knew Jimmy for a long time. Jimmy had military honors at his graveside. I'm sure he was looking down from heaven and was pleased.

Another Vietnam Vet that was very special to me and our entire community was a fellow we all called Smitty. He died some years ago of cancer. I was honored to get to write his eulogy at his memorial service. His best friend in Nashville was his barber, Denny Haynes. I go to church with Denny, and think about what great friends they were every time I see him. Denny's barber shop was an icon on Nolensville Road. We all have to retire sometime, I guess, but Nolensville Road is not the same without Denny.

Smitty was a retired warrant officer. His highly decorated career spanned at least 30 years and three wars. After retirement he returned to Nashville and lived in his old home place until his death. His home was like a time capsule. He had a Naugahyde couch from the 1960s and a small black and white television. The light fixture in the living room was a light bulb with a pull cord. By the end of July, Smitty had every Christmas gift bought and gift wrapped, ready to ship. He learned about organization, efficiency and living simply in the military. When I asked him about updating his house and TV, he just smiled and reminded me he had lived alone for a long time and liked it the way it was. Well, that was true. But his saving habits allowed him to give back so much to his church, lodge, neighbors, family and friends. I saw him give away a new lawn mower to one neighbor and numerous sets of tires to other neighbors.

I know that because I put the tires on their cars. He gave so much. When I tried to encourage him near the end of his life, he told me that he had survived, Korea, the North Pole, war plans in Washington, and two helicopter crashes, but he knew he would not defeat this enemy. He wanted me to know that he had donated his body to medical science. Any remains left were to be buried at Arlington. He served his country, making a difference even after his death. God bless that hero.

I have a good friend and customer named Mel that grew up on a farm. His family was in the feed and fertilizer business. Since my early career was in the tire department for a farm supply company, we hit it off right away. I am going to tell you a little about Mel's military career, our friendship, and a couple of his stories, and then I have a story to tell about my experience in the feed business. My friend Mel has so many stories. Sometimes I try to tell one and I can hardly get it out, I'm laughing so hard! One of my favorites is about the job Mel took after college at a feed and supplement distribution warehouse here in Nashville. From time to time the warehouse was broken into. The alarm company would call Mel to bring a key and let the police in to attend to the break-in. There were so many dangers in the warehouse. The police would use K-9 dogs to help with capture of the vandals. Behind one of the offices there was a small bathroom. I mean small. If you had to do #2, you had to pull your britches down and back into the room and then shut the door. Well the police dog was searching the building and the perpetrator was in the little bathroom with his head sticking out, looking for the dog. The dog went right to him and when he got his head through the door of the tiny bathroom, the door shut. There was the intruder and the dog together in that tiny bathroom. I can only imagine the robber begging for help. The police could not get the door open as it was blocked by the two inside. When they finally did get it open, the vandal had ninety dog bites. I bet he never did that again.

Mel joined the Air Force and learned to fly c-130 planes and rose to the rank of colonel. Before his first deployment to Iraq, he asked me to attend to any vehicle issues his wife and kids had while he was gone. He wanted me to treat them like I treated my own family. I assured him I would. He flew many missions in Afghanistan as well. His military career is over now, but he continues to serve as an official with the FAA. God bless that hero. No one worked any harder than Mel, but his hard work paid off with a great military career. I'm proud to call Colonel Mel Overton my friend.

Before I tell you about six other military heroes, I'll tell you my feed story as I promised. After high school, I worked at the farm supply store. I sold tires and auto service. I thought I would sell feed when I started, but while I never sold any feed, I did get to handle a bunch of it one day. We had an old man who worked for us that had a job kind of like a county agent, or maybe like a customer field relations guy. I never quite figured out his job or position. One day the manager asked me to help him resolve a feed problem. I got to drive a big two ton dump truck and follow this man to a customer's dairy farm. The problem was that some medicated hog feed got mixed up with some dairy feed. It was delivered to his silo and fed to his dairy cattle. Many gallons of milk were lost and the silo had to be emptied. The old fellow told me my job was to empty the silo one feed bag at a time, put the feed in the back of the two ton truck and return it to the warehouse. We got started about 10:00 a.m. He showed me what to do for the first five or six bags and then he talked to the dairy farmer, who wasn't very happy by the way, until about noon. Then he left. Before leaving he told me to stay until the job was done.

I put the bag under the shoot, hit the button, feed would drop into bag. When it got full, I hit the button to cut it off. I would then tie the bag and load it onto the truck. When they were all lined up across the back of truck, I climbed up on the truck and dragged the bags to the front of the truck for stacking. I continued this process until the silo was empty about midnight. I never touched another feed bag ever. I also was never thanked by the agent or the dairy farmer for my efforts that night.

Looking back, I learned that mistakes are going to happen occasionally. And it is not always the one who makes the mistake that has to clean it up. I also learned that no matter what the task is, don't give up. I think the manager realized what a huge task that was. He always showed me kindness and always seemed to have confidence in my abilities and willingness to work hard. Often, when I was working on rear tractor tires, the manager helped me finish the job. What that taught me was that he wouldn't ask me to do something he himself wouldn't do. Thinking about my friend in the feed business made me think of that story and the lessons it taught me. That night of hard work paid off because of the lessons I learned about people. I could not have paid money for a better lesson— besides I got seven hours of overtime!

I am always proud of young people. The ones that work for me and the ones I come in contact with in the community. The young service men interviewed during the war in Iraq were just kids, and they were truly impressive. I watched one such young fellow grow up, and I sold him his first set of tires. He joined the Marines. I kept up with his career when his parents came into the shop. His work in the Marines was so impressive that he is now assigned to Marine One. Wow! He works with the President! His hard work will continue to pay off. God bless that young Marine for his service.

I sold another young man his first tires. He is a young colonel in the Air Force. He led his group of stealth bombers to deliver the first round of ordinance over Bagdad the night the war started. God bless that young officer. We have a soldier that he and his family does business with us, that has served several tours in Iraq. When he got home he was promoted to Brigadier General for the Army. What an accomplishment, especially when he started out as an enlisted man and worked his way up to General. I know he has done some amazing acts of kindness for some of the wounded that served under him. One of the young soldiers lives in a neighboring county, and was very seriously wounded. The General worked very hard to keep the young man encouraged and to teach him to be an encouragement to other soldiers facing challenges. The young soldier spoke to other wounded soldiers at Walter Reed Army Hospital to offer encouragement. God bless General Jeff Holmes and the young soldier for their hard work and love for our country.

The pacific commander for the Air Force is a four star General, stationed at Hickam Field, Hawaii. I had the honor to work on his son's car. I got a call from the General to add some things to the service we were performing on his son's car, and enjoyed our phone conversation very much. What a well-spoken man. I bet if I asked the General what he is most proud of, it would not be the hardware on his shoulders or the ribbons on his chest. It would be his family, and the men and women he gets to serve with every day. God bless General Gary North. I must tell you about Joe Davis. Joe has been my friend and client (when he was still driving), for many years. Joe served in the Army in WWII. He fought the Germans in Casino. He was a retired postal worker and reminded me of my dad in many ways. He enjoyed raising a garden and giving away the vegetables he raised, just like my dad. He, too, as he got older, got emotional when talking about the war. Many people might think Mr. Davis has some strange views about life, but I connected with him very well. Mr. Davis called me one day and asked my opinion about him giving a donation toward the WWII memorial in Nashville. Some of his family didn't quite understand why it mattered so much to him. He valued and asked my opinion on his donation. I told him that he had always provided well for his family and I asked him if he felt like he could spend that kind of money without affecting his and his wife's standard of living. He said yes. I then asked if he

Practice due diligence, and never give up. Hard work leads to success.

worked and saved that money and if it would bring him joy to give it away. He said yes, and I told him my opinion. God bless Joe Davis and his service to our nation and his willingness to give so others may never forget.

Auto part salesmen used to call on us. They would go to our stock room, write up our orders for stock and have them delivered. Then they would put the order on the shelf and reorder what we had sold. This is done different today, but in the old days it worked pretty well. We had a parts salesman that worked for Chilton's Auto Parts named Milton Ferrell. We called him Milton from Chilton. After Milton retired, I pulled his car into the shop one day and noticed two model airplanes on the car seat. I asked if he was working on them with his grandchildren. He told me that he was and that he used to fly planes like that for the Navy in WWII. All these years and I never knew that. I asked him why he didn't fly commercially after the war. He said that during the war our country needed pilots. They asked him to fly and he did. After the war he returned to his parts selling job. He received the Navy Cross for all the missions he flew. Wow! God bless Milton.

You reap what you sow.

I could go on and on with great stories of hard work and success. But you get the picture. I learned early on that you only get out of something what you put in. You reap what you sow. Don't worry about how others work. Continue to stay the course. Practice due diligence, and never give up. Hard work leads to success.

My Mom and Dad in our Dickson home

MOTIVATION

The definition for Motivation is: The force that drives humans to achieve their goals.

In an earlier chapter I mentioned that my family motivated me. Well, that is correct. I can't think of anything that would motivate a person more. You want to be a success to provide for your family. To be a good husband and a good father you must be a good provider. That responsibility should be a good motivator for any one. As I stated earlier, my dad wanted me to be a lineman. I was afraid to climb, but I wanted his blessing and I wanted him to be proud of my accomplishments in the profession I chose. That was a good motivator for me to work hard and be successful. I have always believed in hard work and in leading by example. My boys always saw two things from me: I was never lazy; I went to work every day. And I always loved their Mother and treated her properly. They knew where I would stand on most issues. My example will give them a good foundation to start their lives. I wanted them to know that they and their mother were important to me. Their mother did a good job teaching them all the other important stuff!

Staying motivated and on top of the world is a daily assignment. Granted, the older I get, the more motivation I need to tackle some projects.

Every morning Miss Kim walks me to the door to see me off. She makes sure I have my lunch, phone, store keys and my book satchel. Some men carry a brief case, some carry a man-purse; I happen to carry a book satchel. When I was a little kid in the first grade we carried book satchels to school. Now kids carry backpacks. I used to ask the boys when they were getting ready for school where their book satchel was. They always got a kick out of that.

I always kiss Miss Kim goodbye at the back door and tell her I'll be back in a little while. Most of the time it's 12 hours later. I usually try to do something to make her laugh or smile before I pull off. Brad has a cargo van with a lift gate to haul his antique organs for shows and recording sessions. Both the boys and I like to drive that thing. When you start it up the radio turns wide open on its own. There was a bluegrass cassette in the radio that Brad had been listening to one morning. I drove his van to work that day and the bluegrass music was blasting so I got out and did a little dance for Miss Kim. I slapped my leg like the buck dancers do and she really liked that. Some weeks later her mother visited us from Kentucky, and my dancing abilities came up in conversation. When asked to perform, I told my mother-in-law that I just wasn't motivated right then, but maybe some other time.

My mother never went out in public without being dressed nicely and having her hair fixed and her makeup on. She took pride in her appearance. Miss Kim is that way. She always wants to look nice. One morning at the driveway I was getting ready to pull out and go to work. Kim was just inside the garage door and had started to close the door. She still had on her pajamas. She would never even go to the mail box or let anyone see her in her pajamas. She couldn't see him but the garbage man was coming down the driveway. I blew the horn and motioned for her to come out to my truck like I forgot something. About that time the garbage man rounded the corner in his truck. Boy, she got in that garage and shut the door in a hurry. Little funny things like that help keep me motivated to get in the truck every day. I sure am lucky to have that kind of motivation.

INSPIRE

The definition for inspire is: To influence, move or guide.

We are all influenced by people in our lives. Some influence, good or bad, will last all our lives. As we go through different stages of our lives we are constantly being influenced by others and our surroundings. Any time I have been inspired it seems it has always been for the good. Many times I have been influenced and that has not always been for the positive. Any time I allowed myself to be influenced in a negative manner; I always paid a high price. Any time I was influenced in a positive manner, it always seemed to pay big dividends and yield some type of rewards. As mentioned earlier, no matter where we are or what we are doing, someone is watching. Sometimes we can be an inspiration to folks and we never know it.

I have had so many people be an inspiration to my career and to my personal life. Some people I knew and others I never met but their stories inspired me. Some inspirations came in the form of sayings and slogans. One of my favorite slogans came from the

Shriners: "NO MAN STANDS SO TALL AS WHEN HE STOOPS TO HELP A CHILD."

Vince Lombardi once said, "WINNING ISN'T EVERYTHING, IT'S THE ONLY THING."

My parents were a great inspiration to me and my siblings. Anything we ever needed they always found a way for us to have it. My mother had a fifth grade education but was the smartest women I ever knew. There was not much she couldn't do or couldn't figure out.

During ice storms, my dad climbed icy utility poles to restore downed power lines. Dad could raise a vegetable garden like you can't imagine. He could fix the car and paint the house. There wasn't much he couldn't do either.

After World War II, my oldest siblings were young and my mother wanted them to have matching Easter outfits for Easter Sunday, but she and my dad didn't have the money to buy them. My mother improvised. Many of the servicemen kept their dress uniforms after the war to show off in years to come. Now my mother figured the war was over and dad wouldn't need his anymore, so she cut it up and used the material to make my brother and sister matching Easter outfits.

Daddy had an old white '53 Chevy. He wanted a black one. We didn't have the money for that; we didn't even have the money for a paint job. Dad was out of town working and my mother and siblings pulled his car in the garage, taped the windows, hand sanded and painted his Chevy with a vacuum cleaner.

This story is a good example of how my parents overcame challenges and came up with solutions to any issue. These stories and others are constant Inspirations to me. I think I inherited my problem-solving abilities.

Family, friends, customers, people I see in passing are all inspirations. I try daily to recognize and use them in my business and personal life.

RECOGNIZE

The definition of recognize is: To acknowledge formally.

When our customers come in the door, no how many balls we have in the air, we try our very best to at least greet them. We let them know that we know they are here and they are important to us. If I'm on the phone, I will wave or smile or both to let them know I'll be right with them. I am not quite as good as I used to be, but I try to acknowledge every client by name. Earlier in the book I mentioned how important it is to be recognized by name.

Our co-workers and employees like to be recognized. My work days are usually pretty busy and so are my staff's work days. There is not much time to be patting each other on the back. However, I find ways to work recognition in most days while at the shop. As I go from the office to the alignment bay at the other end of the shop, I'll tap a shoulder occasionally and say good job. Many times that's all it takes. I try to let everyone know when they are really doing well. Then when I have to do some correcting, it is received a little easier and more constructively, and we are all better off—the employee, the company, the customer, and me.

Young son Brad helped Aaron in the office when I was recently away from the store for a few weeks. One of the fellows in the shop said it would be good to have some hoodies with our logo to wear at work on cool days, when a jacket or coat might be too much. We have ordered them in the past, and just hadn't thought about it recently. Brad told him he would work on the idea. Brad gathered the suppliers, cost and delivery dates and presented them to me. I thought it was splendid. One fellow had the idea. Brad and Aaron took the idea, presented it properly, with all the facts, got it approved, and recognized all the fellows in the shop with a little swag.

When the crowd is right, I like to recognize customers for their accomplishments in front of other customers. I like to see customers do business with each other. Many business relationships started in our waiting area. That is great!

REWARD

The definition for reward is: Objects or events that make us come back for more.

Rewards are important to everyone. We want our customers to come back. We want lifetime customers. In business, repeat business and loyalty is what makes our business successful. In order for that to happen, we must reward customers with the best products and service possible. If we give them the "wow factor," we've rewarded them. My reward is when our staff does well, and the customer returns and becomes a regular.

We try to do little things to reward our employees for their hard work and efforts, beyond their compensation package. A few years ago, Miss Kim and I were at a department store just before school started. At that time Brad was still in college, so I had forgotten how stressful that time of year was for young parents. I observed two young parents with their school list. They were just about on each other's last nerve. The young father was looking for things on his list and the young mother was doing the same. I overheard the lady fussing and the father replied that he was just trying to help. They both were stressed.

When Kim and I left the store, I shared with her what I had witnessed. She reminded me what a stressful time it was for us, too, and what a strain that time of year was on the family budget. Monday morning I gave every employee a back to school bonus to help offset the expenses for those with kids. The ones that didn't have school age children also received a back to school bonus so they could buy themselves something as well. It was a small token of our appreciation to reward them for their hard work and to let them know that Kim and I appreciate them and their families. I share this because many companies give Christmas bonuses to help with the expense of that time of year; and we do, too. But financial rewards are appreciated at other times of the year, too. If you're a business owner, we encourage your company to offer a back to school bonus, like we have done in the past.

OPPORTUNITY

The definition of opportunity is: A set of circumstances that makes it possible to do something.

I could write an entire book on this subject. Our great nation is just full of opportunities for our families, our communities and our businesses. Coach Bryant used to say that every day we have an opportunity to write a new page. The great coach was so right.

The opportunities my business has given my family and me are just endless. We are all given opportunities in life that are endless as well. It's up to us to take advantage of all opportunities that present themselves to us. Don't waste a single one. I've wasted many, but I sure want to be careful not to continue to make that mistake. I want to make a difference.

When I speak to groups, I never know how I am going to connect with the crowd. Some talks go better than others. Sometimes I light up the audience with my stories and words of encouragement. Sometimes I wonder if anyone is paying attention. Every time I step up to the podium, on stage or in front of a camera, I worry how it is going to turn out. Why would anyone lay it all on the line and take a chance when you may not do a good job or you choke a little? Well, if they all get it, and we connect and enjoy our time together, it's worth it. If it doesn't go quite as well, but just one person in encouraged by something I have said, then it's worth it.

I hope this book is received that way. If it sells a bunch of copies, I'm flattered. If it doesn't sell at all, maybe I can give a copy to someone who will be encouraged by something I have written. Then it would have been worth the time and effort and any risk of any kind. Let us all try our best to never let good opportunities pass us by.

REPUTATION

The definition for reputation is: The beliefs or opinions that are generally held about someone or something.

I've heard people say, "I don't care what people think." I've said that, too. But usually, this isn't really true. At the end of the day, many times our good reputation, our integrity, and our good name are all we have left. So I think it is very important to protect our personal and professional reputation. It takes a lifetime to build and can be destroyed in an instant. It's my opinion that we should guard and protect it.

In business the last thing I want is an unfavorable reputation. My staff and I work very hard to keep our reputation spotless and a bright shining example of what a business should be. That does come at a price. It is expensive to conduct business right, however the outcome is priceless.

In today's computer age, we want positive things written about us in social media and Internet. Building and protecting your reputation is also done one step at a time. Building and protecting our reputation is a great motivator for doing the right thing.

I told a group one time if everyone would do the right thing we wouldn't need as many police officers or many jails. Of course everyone won't do the right thing all the time. But if every business would strive to do just that, it would make it easier to keep their customers. And likewise, if all customers would do the right thing, it sure would make it easier on businesses. It's expensive to do the right thing; however, it pays big dividends.

Like I tell our staff, if you do the right thing, you can't be wrong.

In this chapter about good reputations and doing the right thing, and since this is a book all about the footsteps of life and the impact we make on each other's lives, I want to share with you a little about the doctor that delivered me and my sister Mitzie. His name was Dr. Jimmy Hayes.

My older three siblings were delivered at home; Mitzie and I were the only two delivered in a hospital. As the years have gone by I have heard many stories about Dr. Hayes. From everything I've heard, he must have been a character. I had the opportunity to meet Dr. Hayes at a Shriner's meeting before he died.

When Kim and I lived on Edmondson Pike in Nashville, we had a neighbor named Mrs. Cunningham whose late husband Speedy was a highway patrolman. Mrs. Cunningham was a nurse and had worked with Dr. Hayes. Most of her stories are funny and so are the ones about her times working with Dr. Hayes.

She told me that Dr. Hayes and his wife had vast real estate holdings. One of those properties was a cemetery, and Dr. Hayes moved his office from Church Street in Nashville to the cemetery property. Now that just doesn't seem like a good business move to me. For that doctor's patients to go see him at a funeral home property, you know he was something special. Maybe it was a genius idea. Move out of a building you can charge more rent for, move into a building that you might have a hard time renting to anyone else, and create traffic and promote the funeral home business all at the same time!

Dr. Hayes' friend Mr. Pugh took care of the plumbing needs for his properties. The late Mr. Pugh and his wife had about eight kids—Dr. Hayes probably delivered them, too. When one of the Pugh kids got sick, Dr. Hayes would come to their house and give all the kids a shot with the same needle. As the years went by, Mr. Pugh's daughter prepared the plumbing business statements and questioned her dad on the amount being billed to Dr. Hayes. Mr. Pugh would not charge Dr. Hayes very much because when Mr. and Mrs. Pugh were building their business with all those children Dr. Hayes never charged them over $5 for a house call and shot. Dr. Hayes knew they were struggling and was always kind to Mr. Pugh. Later Mr. Pugh was able to repay that kindness. You see both of these businessmen had a heart of service, and did the right thing. They touched lives, made a difference, and left behind some beautiful life lessons.

Mrs. Cunningham told me if anyone in my family ever got sick and was hospitalized, she would come and be a private nurse at no cost. I value her as a client and a friend more than she will ever know.

I hear funny stories from customers nearly every day. A collage of those stories would make a pretty good book by itself. Maybe volume two was just born.

The great thing about stories is that like jokes, one leads to another. A good example is as follows.

My friend Bama Jim Johnson introduced me to Paul McCullough. We call him Mack. Mack has a talking bird. Talking birds mimic the voices of the ones they are around the most. This bird sounds just like Mack. Mack taught that bird to say, "Go to Bass Tire." So we shot a TV commercial with Mack, his grandson Brandon and the bird. It was so funny!

My friend and customer Charlie Cooper and his wife Ann saw the commercial and shared a story about Ann's parents, the McMurray's, and their talking bird. They were in the dairy business and milked cows. Their bird sounded just like Mrs. McMurray. When Mr. McMurray was in the dairy barn milking and that bird yelled, "Mac, telephone!" it sounded like Mrs. McMurray was calling him to the phone. He would stop milking, run to the house to find Mrs. McMurray on the front porch sweeping. Now that is funny to me.

No finer folks than Charlie and Ann Cooper. Charlie loves to fish. Aaron and I keep Charlie's boat trailer road- worthy. After Charlie had returned from a recent fishing trip and shared his fishing stories with me, I started thinking about fishing. I bet it has been twenty years since I have gone fishing. I know I have not been since our kids were little.

Some years ago I was on a motorcycle ride with some friends and clients and I took them to Kim's hometown of Salem, Kentucky. We went on to Paducah and to Unionville, Tennessee and spent the night. The next morning we went to Reelfoot Lake and saw the eagle sanctuary and the majestic beauty of Reelfoot. I met a young man at a boat dock and asked him about the fishing at the lake. He advised me to get a guide if I wanted to fish for crappie in Reelfoot. He also mentioned the abundance of cotton mouth snakes. Well after that, I haven't been too anxious to renew my fishing hobbies.

But the years have gone by, so I recently tried to recruit our son Bradley, who is a shooter, to take his shot gun and side arm to watch for snakes while I fished Reelfoot, but he declined as he was too busy. I shared that story in the office the other day and Bob Garner, a friend and client, shared his Reelfoot story with me and the customers in the waiting area. Bob said he had a friend, a captain on the highway patrol, who fished Reelfoot Lake with his good friend Mr. High. Now High had a fondness for Jack Daniels Black Label. They caught a lot of crappie one night and they heard some bull frogs croaking around some Cyprus trees and the captain told High to turn the trolling motor toward the Cyprus trees and get some frogs, since frog legs would go good with their fish for supper. High reached into the water to retrieve a frog and when he pulled it out a big cotton mouth snake had a hold on the frog. The captain told High to squeeze hard behind the snake's mouth. He opened the cooler and the snake dropped the frog right in the ice chest. In the meantime the snake had coiled its body around High's arm. High asked the captain how he was going to get the snake off his arm without being bit. The captain said, "Hold his head over here," and he poured some of High's Jack Daniels down that snake's mouth. The snake relaxed and High gently turned the snake loose in the lake. About 20 minutes later High felt something hit him in the back of the neck and the snake had brought him two more frogs. Bob had me going on that one until the end.

David Smith is a bass player that trades with us and lives in nearby Dickson, Tennessee. He bought a farm there and raises horses. We were talking last year of the extreme drought we had. He said it had been so dry at home that he had caught two catfish from his pond and they both had ticks on them.

I think these stories are so funny that I wanted to share them with you. In today's busy world with our non-stop fast paced work environment, it is such a treat to pause and share laughter with one another.

MIRRORS AND IMAGE

The image of Bass Tire is very important to Kim and me. Kind of like protecting your personal reputation, protecting your business image is very important. Our building image is important, as well as our staff image. First impressions are very important.

Sometimes one shot is all you get. If there are any wrinkles in our business, we sure don't want them to show. After work we are going to get the old iron out and get those wrinkles out. The image we want to send our customers home with is one of complete satisfaction, and the feeling they were treated professionally and fairly. We want them to refer their friends and family.

If I'm going to reflect a good image, I need to start with a good mirror. When I look in the mirror the image I see must be a good reflection of the key items I have outlined in this book.

Troy Mills, a fourth generation Bass Tire customer, made this for a school project. Notice how he modeled his logo after ours. What a compliment to our business!

ENCOURAGEMENT

I always mention encouragement when speaking to groups. I talk about that a lot. Life is hard and it is easy to get discouraged, which can create all kind of problems. Miss Kim is a constant encourager to me and others. So many people have had such an encouraging impact on my life. My preacher talks about encouragement from the pulpit. It is that encouragement that makes me want to be a constant encourager, too.

One of the smartest guys I know is a fellow named Larry Kloess. Larry was a hospital administrator in his working career. He is a believer and a polished and well-spoken man with a gentle demeanor. Larry doesn't know it, but he has been an encourager to me and has made a positive impact on my life. I told Larry one time that I should have gone to law school, medical school and politics school so I could have figured out the solutions for many problems. But that didn't happen, so I had to rely on my friends in various fields to guide me from time to time. He continues to take my calls and help me with issues. I know I have worried that man to death sometimes. God bless him.

EMPLOYEES

Our staff is our most expensive asset, as well as our most valuable asset. They have made us shine and I'm so proud of each one. We have had some great successes. Some employees have resigned to try other endeavors. I'm very proud of their accomplishments. We have had some start their own businesses. We have had a few pass away. That is hard for every small business, because you work so closely with your staff every day, and spend so much time with them they become like family, so death is always tough.

We hired a young man years ago to operate our service truck. He had worked on heavy equipment in the Army. He was married and had a two year old child. He was from Montana and looked like Arnold Schwarzenegger. He worked out before coming to work, worked our truck hard during the day and sometimes worked as private security officer at night. His work ethic was impeccable. He resigned to attend college full time. I sure hated to lose him, however with his work ethic and the proper education, I knew he would go far. He earned a doctorate in physical therapy and became an administrator for some hospitals in the central part of our country. I am very proud of him.

I couldn't write my life's work story and include a chapter on employees and not tell you about Dwight. When we were in our first Bass Tire location, I noticed a man walking by every day. He just kind of showed up. He was medium to small in stature and had coal black hair. I asked one of the boys who he was. They told me he was living in a van in the lot behind the store. I went around back to see and sure enough it looked like someone was living in a Dodge Caravan. The next day I was in front of the shop and I saw him again. I called out to him and asked him his name. He walked over to our lot and he had the deepest blue eyes, no teeth, and a very gentle and kind demeanor. I asked if he was homeless and if he really wanted to live like that or if he wanted a job and a place to live. I asked if he thought he could do our kind of shop work, and he said he thought he could. I told him to get himself together and we would give it a try and see how it went. He came to work the next morning. I could tell he was a hard worker and would learn fast.

Dwight had lived a hard life and was older than the other boys in the shop. But he gave it all he had and gave many years of service to our company. When he had been working for us a few days, I began to think about helping him with his living arrangements. I received a phone call from Sally Nelson, an elderly lady customer friend that lived across the street next to the parsonage of Woodbine Cumberland Presbyterian Church. Miss Sally had a two story house with an upstairs apartment. The girl that had rented Miss Sally's apartment for many years got married and moved out.

Miss Sally asked if I knew anyone that wanted to rent her apartment. I told her Dwight's story, and said if she would rent to him I would monitor the situation. Dwight rented from Miss Sally until she sold her house and moved to assisted living.

We moved into our new building, and later that year business dropped off some. Dwight asked to see me after work. He told me that he knew business had been off a little lately, and he had about eight pay checks he had not cashed yet. He asked me if I needed them. Wow! That tells you what kind of heart Dwight had. I told Dwight that the retail business was that way sometimes, and we prepared as a company for those type of swings and to go ahead and cash his checks. I told him how much I appreciated his sincerity.

Dwight had told me about his parents. His mother was still living at that time, but his father was deceased. He showed me a letter from the White House mailed to his mother from Mamie Eisenhower. Dwight's dad had served under General Eisenhower in WWII. When Dwight was born, his folks named him Dwight David Walls, after then President Eisenhower. Dwight's parents sent a letter to the President to let them know they named their son after him and Mrs. Eisenhower sent a letter to Dwight's parents to let them know how honored the President was.

Dwight passed away a few years later in his sleep while on vacation. He died from an aneurism. At his funeral service, I told the packed chapel that story. Dwight wasn't destined to lead the nation like the man he was named after, but he sure impacted a lot of lives, including mine. You see Dwight viewed work a little different than most. It didn't matter to Dwight whether it was a

Monday at noon, or Friday at closing time. He treated every job the same. It didn't matter if the car he was working on was a Cadillac or a beater. It didn't matter to Dwight if the customer was the banker or the baker. He treated every job with the same care and completeness. When he knew the customer he would personally thank them, briefly explain what he did and asked them if there was anything else he could do for them. He was something special and you just can't teach that.

One of Dwight's good friends was Clyde Green, the owner and funeral director at Ellis Funeral Home. Many times Dwight helped Clyde work around the funeral home, not for money but just to visit and help his friend. It is rare that funeral directors cry at funerals, but Clyde did.

Dwight was the first to sign up for our 401k, and he had some life insurance. I'm sure if managed properly it was enough to pay for his grandchild's college education. That's quite an accomplishment for a man who was once homeless. I am confident the Lord put Dwight in my path. He was usually the last to leave at the end of the day. When we closed up for the night, I would look at Dwight and ask him if everything was secure. He would say, "You can code and go." I still think of him when Aaron tells me that now. I am a better man for knowing Dwight.

I've had to terminate a few employees through the years and that is always hard. We had one fellow resign and file a worker's comp suit the next week. That was interesting. We went through a time when it was a challenge to get the right personnel in place. It reminds me of a ball team getting the right players. I have found through the years that most personnel issues have a way of working themselves out. The proper staff sure can make my job a lot easier.

BROTHER PAUL DURHAM

There was a famous preacher on Nolensville Road who has gone on to be with the Lord now, but I'm proud to say that we became friends early in my career and stayed friends until he died. Everyone on Nolensville Road knew Brother Paul. If there was anyone who didn't like him, they must not have known him very well, or they might have been jealous.

I learned many lessons from Brother Paul. I didn't always agree with him, even exchanged a few words one time, but I always loved and respected him. Paul figured out early on that the Lord had called him to preach no matter what. Paul became a very successful business man. He had vast real estate, radio stations, funeral homes, a Lincoln dealership, and he was a full-time pastor. He never took a salary for his preaching. I guess he and the Lord had all that worked out a long time ago. We were members of his church for a while. I was inconsistent in my church life in those days. Paul somehow knew exactly how to handle me. I guess he figured the Lord and I would get all that worked out.

Paul dabbled in politics a little. He was on the traffic and parking commission for a while. We sure needed men with Paul's commitment to doing the right thing in our county government.

Brother Paul was sharp. He was very flamboyant and dynamic in the pulpit. There used to be a TV commercial years ago, "When E.F. Hutton speaks, people listen." Paul was that way. When he started to speak he would get your attention and keep it until he was done. When he asked for quiet across the building on Sunday morning, you could hear a pin drop.

I asked Paul to look at the property I was going to buy where our retail store is now. I wanted to make sure there would be no problems with egress, ingress, parking, etc. He said he didn't see any problems. He told me something then I will never forget. He said that he always looked for ways to say yes and tried his best not to say no, especially with traffic and parking, because a vacant piece of property needed to be developed to bring in tax revenue for our city. To me that made a lot of sense. Paul stood firm on his beliefs and never wavered.

Paul loved his family, loved his church and his members, and he loved to make deals and do business. I think his success was due in part because he walked the walk and talked the talk.

At one time Paul wore cowboy boots in the pulpit. I picked up on that, and today I wear boots to church. One Sunday this lady stopped me and commented on my boots and told me that her preacher used to wear boots. It was Brother Paul. I told her he was my inspiration for wearing them. It is a small world.

Kim and I bought a house down the road from Brother Paul. By this time he wore shoes instead of cowboy boots. I often saw him on his mower mowing in suit britches and dress shoes. I teased him about him not having any old shoes, but he told me if he got a call and had to rush to the hospital, he wanted to be able to hop off the mower and get going. Well he meant just that.

Paul always said when the Lord was ready for him he hoped he would be preaching. Well he got his wish. He had a massive stroke at the conclusion of a Sunday service. He sure touched a lot of lives, including mine.

Billy Hill was a senior adult minister on staff with Brother Paul. What a great pair. They enjoyed many years serving the Lord together. Billy called to check on me regularly. He always wanted to know what was going on at the store and in our personal lives. It seemed like he always knew when I needed encouragement. He called me the Monday before he passed away and went to be with the Lord. We talked about his grandson's car needs, and then just visited a while on the phone.

The next day, Billy was picking up trash from the church grounds down the street from his house. It wasn't his church, but he always helped keep the grounds clean. I think it was important to him and just another way to serve, walk and get some quiet time with the Lord. He had a heart attack and died serving the Lord, just like Brother Paul. I told his wife Monte Jo, that he and Paul were working together again. I looked around at the funeral home and saw so many of our customers there. Customers he sent to me in the first place. Bother Billy touched so many lives, and mine, too.

SPIDER ON MISS RUBY

We attended a little church in Madison, Tennessee for a few years. If we had a hundred in church we had a crowd. Our song leader, Tom, was a retired insurance executive. He had a southern gospel quartet. Tom was very well respected in the gospel music circles in Nashville. So we had some really good groups come play for us that were mostly found in big churches.

Our little church was lucky to have Tom. His wife played the piano. After a couple of years we formed a church band. Patsy played the piano, our son Brad played the bass guitar, a fellow named Buddy and me played the rhythm guitar. We opened the service before the announcements and backed up the choir. Brad was about ten years old and a very good musician. He and Patsy would tell me and Buddy what key to play in and we followed along. Those were fantastic times in our church life.

We met a family and became close friends. Many of the funny things that happened at church seemed to involve either them or us. This story I'm about to share with you will probably not help you in your business, but it is too good not to share. After all I have been called the master story teller. In your life you will have funny situations, too. It's just life. I love to hear other people's stories. I often pass them on. Having the ability to tell stories can help break the ice in many business situations. When you get to know folks well enough to share stories, they will enhance your relationships. Some of my stories may help you in business after all.

Brad is still keeping after it, playing on a recording session at MTSU

At the little church in Madison, we had a revival one week. We had a visiting evangelist. With Tom's contacts in the music industry, we had a visiting southern gospel piano player come to play for us on opening night. He played those old hymns fast. It really challenged the church band. We really were on fire that first Monday night. The preacher was introduced and took the pulpit to set the tone for the week. It was truly a good night.

The next night was Tuesday. In the tire business, I often planned to get caught up early and close on time, but sometimes that just doesn't happen. Tuesday night was one of those times. The revival was in the summer. After a 100 degree day at the tire store, I had to go home and shower and change clothes. Brad had something going on and couldn't go that night, and that was a problem for me and Buddy. You see Brad always told us the key to play in. So when Miss Kim and I finally got to church, Tom was wrapping up the last song. Kim and I took a seat and Tom called me up to help finish the last song. I really just wanted to slip in and sit down. I sure didn't want to interrupt the service. The visiting preacher stared at me. I don't think he liked me interrupting the service either. I was lucky I knew what key it was in. When the song was over, I took a seat with Kim in our normal Sunday morning spot. There were three ladies that often sat together just two rows ahead of us. Miss Eva and the lady in the middle was Miss Ruby and Joy on the other side. Miss Ruby's dress had a big white collar. I could see well in those days. I told Miss Kim there was something on Miss Ruby's dress and if it crawled on her collar I was going to get it off. The visiting preacher was just getting started, when the spider crawled on Miss Ruby's collar. I jumped up and leaned over that pew and knocked the spider off. Of course that scared her and I said, "Spider!" And those three ladies gave that spider the pew! The entire church turned around to see what was going on. The ladies were in the aisle, I was standing up looking embarrassed, and I had disrupted the service again. That poor visiting preacher was really proud of me for knocking that spider around. My friend, Randy was laughing. He knew I had done something before he even turned around. I looked at him and said, "Spider on Miss Ruby!" Order was restored. At the end of the service I asked the visiting preacher if he wished I had stayed home. He said he sure did and smiled.

There are so many more stories about all the funny things that happened while attending that little church. Great people and fond memories.

If time permits, I'll share some more church stories later.

LADY-FRIENDLY BUSINESS

Recently, I have been receiving physical therapy. The therapists are all ladies. The other day another long-time Nolensville Road businessman was there for rehab on his shoulder. We visited and the ladies figured out what I did for a living. One asked if we were a good place for a lady to take her cars for repairs. I answered, "Yes, because I have a sweetie and three sisters, and I would be in big trouble if we weren't lady-friendly." Some types of businesses seem to intimidate some people.

A garage environment carries the stereotype that it is a business for male customers. Many years ago that may have been the case. Now days we see just as many ladies as men taking care of vehicles. One of these days I am going to get the proper software so I can look at the statistics. I base my thoughts on the number of ladies that wait in our waiting room. Some days we have all guys waiting and other days it seems like all ladies. But certainly we have a good mix.

It is important for me to see that everyone that enters our door feels comfortable. We have a nice waiting area and plenty of coffee and sometimes donuts when I'm not on a low carb diet. I hear some ladies say, "I'm just a Woman," or "Do you think so and so told me that about my car because I'm a woman?" I never ever want women to feel that way at Bass Tire, and neither does Miss Kim.

Some customers, including ladies, like to know how worn out components work. Some could care less. Most of the time, men or women, our customers want to know four things:

What is wrong with the vehicle?
What is the cost to repair it?
How long will it take to repair?
When will it be ready?

Regardless of whether the customer is male or female, we tell them what is wrong in a professional manner and try not to use industry jargon that can be difficult to process. We always try to explain service issues in a way that is not condescending.

So, yes, it is important to be lady-friendly but fellow- friendly, too.

Mr. Bob Brennan was a good friend who has gone on to live with the Lord. He was well-traveled and made his living in the magazine business in its heyday. Mr. Bob was a gentleman to all. He not only was a great business man but published many different types of magazines. He knew a lot about a lot of different things.

Each month Mr. Bob had a section in the front of his magazines called "Words from the Editor". He was so kind to mention my company in that section. It was nice to get the plug, but what he said meant so much to me. He said if any young person was contemplating entering the business world, he should sit in our showroom for a little while and see how we did business. He went on to say that we gave all our customers the same respect, whether they were princes or paupers. Yes, we are lady-friendly.

Every holiday, the first card I received was from Mr. Bob. I miss him as my friend and client.

GOOD CUSTOMERS MAKE GREAT FRIENDS

When I refer to a client as a friend, I am correct. If I know someone well enough to tell a story about them, they probably are a friend. If they are your true friend, they are going to be a customer. I have run into people in restaurants, or at ball games or somewhere else in the community. Sometimes Aaron runs into someone and he tries to tell me who they were by saying they used to buy tires from me. Well, where is he buying them now? Did he move off? Was he just passing through? The ones that never waiver and stay with us are very special friends, and I don't take them for granted one moment.

We have many commercial accounts. Many of the employees from those commercial accounts bring their personal vehicles to us. Jack Heldman was an All American basketball player from the 1951 Vanderbilt team who owned a food brokerage company in town. At the highlight of his business, we had every food broker in town. I think Jack and his staff got us all that business.

Two members of Jack's staff still trade with us today. One is Tommy Douglas, who is now retired, and the other is Howard Harris. Tommy is a little older than me and Howard is a little younger. Both men are dedicated family men whom I respect and apprcciate very much. Both have been customers and friends a long lime. I know of some of the struggles that both men have had to endure professionally, and I certainly admire the way they depended on their faith to get them through.

Jack Heldman was a good influence on these two men. Jack had a big, competitive, strong personality. He could be a little intimidating. I was scared to death of Jack at first, and then I realized he was a gentle, caring family man that was a good businessman with a passion for what he did. Jack expected that same passion from his staff. As I have grown older, I understand that now more than ever.

I guess if everyone who ever traded with us was a current customer I could not get them all in. But I sure would like to try to figure out how. I wonder if my Pastor ever feels that way. In my opinion he is a super preacher. I think he is one of the best at what he does. But if every person that ever heard Brother Gene preach was a church member, we could not get them all in either. I guess he has had people say he used to be our preacher. Well, who is their preacher now? People move on to other businesses, no matter how good we and our staff are, or how good our products and service are. But I tell our staff to do what we do and be the best at it. We may not retain all of our customers, but we sure are going to try. Our shop is pretty full every day.

We had a lady come in from the physical therapy clinic I was telling you about earlier. She told my wife she had never received service like we gave her. Speaking of our service, my wife told her that's what we do.

I still have many of the friends I made when I first came to the city to work. A couple of those friendships I can't write about. Some of the stories I will share, but some I won't. Some I have been in trouble with Miss Kim before and there is no need to get in trouble with her again. I don't want to get my buddies in trouble!

My friend James worked for a family electrical distributorship in Nashville right after high school. I worked for a family tire dealership in Nashville. Our two bosses were friends. I'm sure our names came up from time to time when our bosses visited.

I first met James Turner at the full-service service station where we worked weekends and nights. The first Sunday we worked together he just about worked me to death. I wasn't going to let him out work me and he wasn't going to let me out work him. That worked out good for George Perkins, the man that owned the station. George's little brother David worked with James at the electrical supply house during the day and worked for George at night at the station. The part time crew was David, James and me. We alternated nights and weekends. During busy times we worked together. George used to say he had the best part time crew in town and his part time staff was better than most people's main crew. We all formed a great friendship that is still strong today. For that I am sincerely blessed.

In the early days we went on fishing and camping trips. We had Monday night football chili suppers and we played music together and formed a great bond. As we all got older and married and got busy building our careers, we didn't have as much time to hang out. David married Connie and moved across town. James married Kathy and moved close by. So James and Kathy and Kim and I and the kids took trips together, went racing together and were as close as any two brothers anywhere.

Neither one of us had much money, so we tackled any household project ourselves. We weren't afraid to tackle just about anything. We helped each other and showed off our handiwork to other friends. Our projects included decks, fences, fireplaces, a work shop, two swimming pools and two hot rod vehicles. We also painted two vehicles, installed equipment at Bass Tire, rebuilt a pontoon boat, and installed a water heater. I'm sure there were more, but those are a few that made us proud.

James's motor ran all the time. He never ran out of projects. I think he would be about halfway through with one and already working on the next one in his head. Whenever he was through with a project he had already had the next one worked out. His office was downtown close to where the pro football stadium is located now. He decided to pressure wash and seal all the aggregate on the sidewalk around his building. We worked on it Saturday and Sunday. And we did that project twice.

The company he worked for had customer appreciation dinners at their warehouse. James would set up the tables, do the cooking, and clean up. Of course I would help. Many of James's co-workers and clients became my friends and clients, too. We were networking; we just didn't know it.

James and David enjoyed being around my parents and I enjoyed theirs, too. We are all orphaned now as all our parents have gone on to be with the Lord. Before we all got married, James and David went on a fishing trip across the entire state on their vacation. They spent the night at my folks in Dickson. The next morning my mother cooked a big breakfast of homemade biscuits, eggs, fried potatoes, fried chicken and gravy. They talked about that a long time.

I became very close to David's parents while I worked for his brother in the service station. We called David's dad "Perk," short for Perkins.

Perk was on up in years, but worked 16 hour days at the station. One night about 9:00 p.m., Perk and I were working together, He was in the office where he could man the gas pumps, and I was in the shop preparing to mop the floor. About that time a man pulled up in a Buick Rivera and wanted to check his transmission. I told him I could check his fluid, but the diagnosis of a particular problem would have to be scheduled and checked in during the day. He asked me to check his fluid. In those days, most vehicles used transmission fluid in power steering units. I had used just a little fluid out of a quart in another power steering unit, and I got a funnel, and poured the rest of that quart in the man's tranny. I told the man it would be $2.00. He didn't want to pay it. Looking back I should have thanked him and sent him on his way. But, I wasn't about to let that happen. I was young and in pretty good shape and wasn't afraid of much, so you can just about see where this is going. When I saw the situation escalating I clocked that guy right in the mouth. When he went down I proceeded to wear him out. I was doing pretty darn good until he finally connected a good one and the lights just about went out in Georgia. He got on top of me and was beating the tar out of me, and here came Perk. I told Perk to get the gun and shoot the guy. It seemed like Perk was gone for thirty minutes. When he returned to the fight, he said someone had stolen the gun. Then I told Perk to take his walking stick and hit that guy; he was killing me. Perk popped that guy in the ear with his stick and it gave me a chance to at least get to my feet. The guy took a swing at Perk. Perk caught himself with his walking stick and said, "If you have broke my artificial teeth, you have had it." I couldn't let Perk get hurt, so I fell in on that guy again. He finally broke and ran to his car and backed out on Harding Place. I picked up the $2.00 and told Perk to put it in the cash register. We earned it.

When George returned to help close for the night, there Perk and I were. Perk's glasses were broken. My uniform shirt was just about torn off. Blood was all over my shirt and my eyes were just about swollen shut. My nose was broken, teeth chipped; we were a sight. Miss Kim and I were going together at the time. When I knocked on the door at her apartment about midnight, she thought I had been in a car wreck. I told her I had nearly beaten a fellow to death. In reality, it was the other way around. I never pulled a stunt like that again. That good whipping kept me from starting any more fights. I figured I better learn to be a better negotiator.

That story was one that Perk and I got a lot of mileage out of and told many times. It got better each time we told it.

James' dad Vernon was a funny guy, too. Mr. and Mrs. Turner lived close to the Highland Rim Speedway, and Kim and I went with James, Kathy and Mr. and Mrs.

Turner to the races. Mr. Turner was a good gardener and always insisted we raid his garden. Mr. Turner was like my dad, he could do just about anything. In his working career he was an appliance repairman for Sears. One of my favorite stories about Mr. Turner was about a service call he went on at the residence of Col. Tom Parker. Mr. Turner was working on the washing machine and could feel someone watching him. He looked up and it was Elvis. He was sitting on the floor watching Mr. Turner work. So Elvis and Mr. Turner visited like two old friends catching up while Mr. Turner fixed the washer. Mr. Turner had a gift of being at ease no matter who he was around. He made everyone else feel at ease, too. What a great gift to have. I sure did enjoy both of my friends' dear parents.

During my days with Universal Tire, I was introduced to Herman Brown. Mr. Lovell, one of our vice presidents, sent Mr. Brown to me to balance the wheels on his Cadillac. Many times unusual balance problems would be sent to me. Mr. Brown was old enough to be my father, but we formed a great friendship that lasted until he lost his battle with Alzheimer's disease. Herman had a lot of great stories. Many of them I had heard a hundred times, but I still enjoyed them.

Herman was a big Tennessee fan. Herman and his wife Gerry, had a camper. We bought a camper to go camping and racing. Herman was a big help when we got involved with camping. Our families went camping together. Often we cooked while we were camping and our family and friends would join us for a meal. We really had some good times. For a few years we took our motor homes to Montgomery Bell State Park for the weekend before the kids started back to school after spring break. The kids and I would play army, go to the lake, ride our bikes, and have a blast. Kim's dad gave us a scooter, like a moped and we rode that thing all over the camp grounds. After our evening meal we would build a camp fire and take turns telling tales and stories.

Another friend, Cliff, saw what a good time we had camping and racing and he bought a camper, too, so he could join us.

One time, Cliff asked J.D. Smith to help him drive his motor home back to Nashville after a NASCAR race just outside of Atlanta. J.D. agreed. We followed J.D. Once traffic allowed, we were poking along about 56 mph. I got on the CB radio to ask J.D. why he was driving so slowly. He said Cliff wanted him to drive that speed because his coach got the best fuel mileage at that speed. We were used to letting those things roll on our way home. In a little while J.D. radioed me and said Cliff was asleep and let's go. We opened those big 454 engines and consumed some fuel. Cliff woke up several times and asked J.D. how fast he was going. J.D.'s answer was always the same, 56 mph. Cliff never knew any different.

Cliff and I formed a great friendship. I always enjoyed being around his folks, too. His father retired from the Davidson County Sheriff's Department, and he could tell some great stories. I had the honor to emcee Cliff's parents' golden wedding anniversary. It was a wonderful and fun evening.

Cliff's mother and father both have gone to be with the Lord. They were always so kind to us and all the boys at the shop. Mr. Miller brought us our lunch sometimes. We had a man named Pete work for us years ago. Pete would tell Mr. Miller, "Don't bring me barbecue. It runs up my blood pressure. Bring me a bologna sandwich." I asked Pete what he thought bologna was made out of.

Our friends mean so much to our personal and professional lives. I wouldn't take anything for all the fun times, the laughs and the great relationships. If it weren't for our business our lives may have never touched. Kim and I treasure each and every one of our friends and try to let them know how much they mean to us.

Many funny things happened to one of the families we knew at Madison Baptist Church. There are many stories I can tell about Randy Hodges. His parents were easy to get to know and love as well. Randy is a big ole boy. When facing any challenge, Randy would say, "Pile it on, I have got real big shoulders. You load the wagon and I'll pull it." We hadn't been attending Madison very long, and someone decided we needed a soft drink machine in the fellowship hall so we could sell drinks and raise money for our youth summer camps and different needs. Brad had a school friend he played music with and his friend's grandparents, the Johnsons, had a detached garage they had turned into a recording studio. That had such an impact on Brad and his music future. Kim and I dropped Brad off at the Johnsons house to play music. Mr. Johnson had an old drink machine in front of his garage. When I asked him to help me find one for the church, he gave it to me. I borrowed a trailer and a dolly to take the drink machine to church on Saturday after work. Mr. and Mrs. Hodges had some help lined up to help get it in the building, clean it up, get some drinks in it and see how it worked. Mrs. Martha, Randy's mother, is like Miss Kim. She nearly rubs a hole in stuff cleaning it up. That drink machine was no exception.

Mr. Veachel, one of the deacons, was usually one of the first to church on Sunday mornings. The next morning, Mr. Veachel got there to prepare for Sunday service. The drink box had been on all night. When it got good and cold, snakes came out of the machine. Well Mr. Veachel found them all and turned them loose outside, before the members started to come in. I liked to get to Sunday school a little early because I could visit and have a cup of coffee and donuts. I like to sit next to Ray Hodges and hear his stories, too.

I walked in not knowing anything about the snakes. Ray called me away from the donuts, and wanted to talk to me. He said that he knew I hadn't been coming to church there too long but it was not a church that handled snakes. I said that was good because I was afraid of snakes. He said I must not be because I had brought them to church. I still did not have a clue what he was talking about. When he told me about Mr. Veachel and the snakes, I started looking around at my feet, to make sure there were no stragglers.

A year or two later, Brad broke his wrist playing football. Ray asked Brad if he heard how Ray had broken his finger when he was young and played football. Ray told Brad that they had a wooden bench. He was sitting on the bench and had stuck his finger in a knot hole in the bench. There was a play that ended out of bounds. The bench was turned over while Ray had his finger in it. Ray had a ton of stories just like that.

Randy has been and continues to be a special friend. We watched our boys grow up and we have laughed at each other so much. No matter where we go, when we meet new friends, it is not long until a Bass or Hodges story surfaces.

One of my favorite stories about Randy is when he had a broken ankle. Randy loves bird hunting better than almost anything. Usually twice a year, he travels west to Kansas for a hunting trip. Often the weather is very bad during bird hunting season. He and his family were on a hunting trip when it began to snow. Remember I told you he was a big ole boy; you know a big man is not going to miss many meals. He was going to get some biscuits and slipped on some ice and broke his ankle. He had to have surgery in Kansas before he could come home. When I learned about his situation, I called his cell phone. When I asked how he was doing, he told me his surgery went well, and he was eating chocolate pudding. I offered to take the seats out of my Suburban,

Randy Hodges and myself cutting up at Madison General Baptist Church

put an air mattress in there and come get him, to help get him home. He already had that figured out. The rehab and healing process took many weeks. When he started feeling better, his wife Debra brought him to my office to hang out a while so he could get out of the house and back into some type of routine. He had this big cast on his leg and ankle. He was seated at my desk with his leg under the desk to protect it. There is a lot of traffic in and out of the service office at Bass tire, and he didn't want anyone to hit his foot. He stayed a couple of hours, got tired and called Debra to come get him. If you have ever had a broken bone with a cast for an extended period of time, you know that sometimes an odor can occur from inside the cast. I kept smelling something. I first thought it might be Randy's cast. After he left, I could still smell that smell under my desk where Randy was sitting. I checked the trash can, to make sure that wasn't it. The next day, the smell was no better. I realized it was my own work shoes that had soured. I found another pair at work and threw the old shoes away. I felt bad, blaming my friend, but it sure was funny to me. So I called Randy and began to tell the story. We laughed so much about that. Since then, Miss Kim buys me a new pair of shoes every six months. There are many more stories of our adventures, but I'll save those for later on.

I am sometimes asked the question, who is my best customer? Well of course they all are. I guess the most truthful answer is the customers that have been loyal for the longest period of time. I told you about Charles Adams in an earlier chapter. He is not the oldest in age, but he has allowed me to service his auto needs longer than anyone else. Of course, his personal cars don't bring in the amount of revenue that many of our commercial accounts do, but the years of business and friendship we have shared makes him very special to me. I never take loyalty and friendship lightly. One night in 1978, I was working late in the office at Universal Tire and a man pulled up and knocked on the door. He had a flat. I let him in, fixed the flat and formed a friendship that still last to this day. He has retired from the railroad. I had no idea how important that one after-hours good deed would be to me. My friend's name is Jere Trevethan. Jere knows about value. His family was in the grocery business when he was young. He learned about good customer service in those days. Jere's brother-in-law co-owned an elevator company in town. Jere got us most of that business, which has expanded to the elevator employees and their families. He helped us get some of the railroad business, too, just by telling about our good service.

Of course all of Jere's family does business with us and that really helps us. Jere is one of our best salesmen. Remember our customers are our best salesmen. Our business has snow balled, just from a late night favor.

One afternoon, a local paper wanted to do a piece on our company. Jere was in the store. I answered the interviewer's questions. The store began to get busy and I needed to wrap up the interview, but the interviewer wasn't quite through. So I turned him over to Jere to finish the interview. There is probably no one else but Miss Kim that knows me and our business any better than Jere. He finished the interview so I could wait on customers and did a better job than I could. You see Jere never worried about referring us to his family and friends. He knows we will always do our best and never embarrass him. Some folks are afraid to recommend a business to a friend because they never know how it is going to go. I take pride in the fact that our business is built on referral. Jere and I enjoy going to lunch on Saturdays and catching up. He is very special to me.

My next oldest client is the Jim Sweeney family. Mrs. Sweeney makes banana nut bread at Christmas, just like my grandmother used to make. The third generation of Sweeney's now trade with us. Jim is retired now and does not put the miles on his car like he did when he was working so I don't get to see him as much as I used to, but I sure appreciate his loyalty and friendship and his family.

Christmas time is a special time at our company. We do the Santa TV spots to wish everyone a Merry Christmas and we usually get a little time off, depending on what day of the week Christmas falls on. The food and baked goodies our staff gets from our customers is a little overwhelming, and humbling. We have so many good clients that spoil us and make us goodies just to say thank you and Merry Christmas. The thoughtfulness and love in each of those gifts is appreciated by all of us at Bass Tire. They help make our Christmas even more special. The Christmas cards sent to us each year are displayed on our doors as you enter our showroom. Ever since I was a little kid, I always like to get mail, especially Christmas cards, so I really enjoy them.

We always close on Christmas Eve and Christmas Day. In the early years we tried to work a half a day on Christmas Eve, but we stopped doing that after an interesting series of events one Christmas Eve. In the early nineties, we came to work on Christmas Eve, and had a table set up with goodies like homemade candy and cookies, some Miss Kim had made and some our customers had made. One of the neighborhood ladies had made us a big pot of spaghetti. About 8:00 a.m. a lady wearing a full length mink coat that probably cost more than our monthly salaries combined brought in a Volvo for an alignment. When I waited on the lady, I asked if she wanted any goodies, candy or spaghetti, and she informed me she just wanted her car aligned. I said, "Yes, ma'am," and went on back to work. In the meantime, Mr. Fishburn, a dear old friend and client came in to pay me for tires I had put on his son's truck for Christmas. Mr. Fishburn has passed on now, but what a fine gentleman. He had worked at the Ford Glass plant in his working career. Mr. Fishburn was legally blind. His sight had become so bad, he could no longer drive. He still smoked. At home his wife would put out big dishpans for him to put out his cigarettes, so he wouldn't burn the house down. I asked him as well if he wanted any goodies or candy, and he held his hand out and said for me to pick out some homemade candy and put it in his hand. Now he had a cigarette burning, and the lid was off the spaghetti, so he put his cigarette out in the spaghetti lid. I never said a word, and gave him his candy. He gave me his wallet and told me to get out what I needed to pay for his son's tires, he had purchased for a Christmas gift. After we visited for a while, I walked with him out to his wife's car and said my goodbyes and wished him a Merry Christmas.

In a little while I saw the lady in the mink coat eating a plate of spaghetti. I looked and the lid was back on the spaghetti. I asked Mr. Pearson, my assistant, in the shop, if he had cleaned the cigarette butt out of the lid and he said no. I told him to take that spaghetti away from the lady in the Volvo. I said, "If she gets that butt in a bite of that spaghetti we've had it." He started laughing because he did in fact clean the lid. But that sure shook me up at first.

Early in my Bass Tire career, I was the youngest in the circle of friends that I hung out with when I wasn't working. Car races, football games and dinners are some of the things we enjoyed together with our families when we were not working. One of our friends was a practical joker named Carl Talley. His motor ran all the time and was always thinking up something funny to do to someone.

Earlier I told you about Herman Brown. Carl and Herman were also friends. They played jokes on me and on each other. Someone kept cutting Herman's water off at the meter. Herman would be ready to shower and have no hot water. He would have to get dressed, go to the street take the meter cover off, get a wrench, reach way down in the hole to turn the water back on. It didn't take long for that to get old. Herman told Carl what was happening and Carl made him a steel long-handled water key and painted it red and white, and wrote ROLL TIDE on it. He wrapped it up and gave it to Herman so he wouldn't have to bend over so far to turn the water back on. Herman was a Tennessee big Orange fan.

Carl loaned one of my former employees a dolly hand truck because he was moving. Well he moved alright, quit without notice, moved out of state and never returned Carl's dolly. It really made Carl and me angry. Carl fussed about that dolly till he died. After a stroke, Carl became confined to a wheelchair and could not go on long trips anymore. On a trip to Talladega, Alabama to a car race, Herman came up with a joke to play on Carl. You see the boy he loaned the dolly to was from Alabama. When we got back home, Herman called Carl, like he did every day to check on him. He always made Carl laugh and picked up his spirits. He told Carl that he saw that boy at the race track, using the dolly to carry car parts for the racing teams. He said that Carl had given him the dolly, and he was making more money than he ever had. Carl believed that he really had seen him and was mad all over again.

Later on we went to Birmingham to see Alabama play Tennessee. Herman did it again when he got back. He said he ran into the boy using the dolly to carry equipment for the ball team, and he sure appreciated Carl giving him the dolly. I don't know if he ever told him it was all a joke. I sure miss both of those guys. They meant a lot to me in business and as close friends.

BROKEN WRIST

When I was in the fifth grade, I wanted to play junior pro football, which is like Pop Warner, or pee wee football. I had a Baltimore Colts helmet, watched Johnny Unitas on Sundays, and dreamed of being a punt, pass and kick champion. I wasn't nearly as good as I thought I was. One week in practice, I fell awkwardly during a tackle, and broke my right wrist. Many years later my son Bradley broke his wrist at about the same age, also playing football.

I remember when I broke mine that it was my first experience with health care providers. As I work on this book, I am preparing a customer service video for a group of health care professionals at a local hospital. I think I will share this and one more story about a country doctor I want to tell you about.

When my coach brought me to Dickson Goodlark Hospital to see about my wrist, they made an X-ray, and Dr. Dan Drinnen set my arm and put a cast on it, the first of three casts as the broken bones healed. I was kept overnight, and put in traction. Dr. Drinnen was very well respected in the community and a fine doctor.

We formed a relationship that lasted until after I was grown and moved away.

The next morning, I had my arm up in the air in traction. Before daylight a doctor was making his rounds. He was whistling coming down the hall, and I could hear him talking all the way at the other end of the hall. I think he was so loud so his patients would know he was coming and they would be awake when he hit their room. My door was open and he looked in as he went by and turned around. He came into my room and wanted to know what had happened to me. He looked at the cast which covered my fingers and asked who put it on. I answered him, and he said he was going to cut some of it off. He told the nurse who was with him to get a saw. They returned and I was scared to death, wondering if the saw was going to cut me. I was also scared because the doctor was a big man, loud, cussed a little and had cow manure on his boots. He wasn't even my doctor. So he cut part of my cast off at about the knuckle line where I could wiggle my fingers. He asked, "Isn't that better?" Then he dropped the saw on the bed, and went on his way.

That doctor was none other than Dr. Jimmy Jackson, a fine doctor and surgeon. Dr. Jimmy had been a battlefield surgeon in the military. He was rough on the outside, but big hearted, and respected in the community. Dr. Jimmy was a colorful and talented individual. He practiced medicine, helped run a hospital, farmed, raised cattle, and made sorghum molasses and sold it in the lobby of the hospital. Little did I know that a year later, I would be seriously injured in a snow sledding accident. The skill of Drs. Jimmy, Dan Drinnen, BJ Smith and

Shannon Curtis and their surgical team would save my life in that country hospital in Dickson.

I was in the hospital for many weeks. All four doctors saw me daily on their rounds. One day I asked one of the doctors to remove my IV. Dr. Jimmy came in the next day and ordered it back in. In those days I thought I might enter the health care profession to help others, too. But something happened that day to change my mind. A young nurse tried to get the IV started, but my veins were playing peek-a-boo. And here came Dr. Jimmy, which made the young nurse nervous and made her job more difficult. Dr. Jimmy cussed a little and decided he would put the IV in my arm. The IV fluid was in a big glass bottle that had a hook on the end to hang on the pole. A plastic tube came out of it. Dr. Jimmy had a hard time with the IV, too, and he began to get agitated. He told the young nurse to move out of his light. She was holding the bottle up and kept moving around Dr. Jimmy until the tube was coiled around his neck!

Well he was really mad then. The young nurse would have quit if she could have, but Dr. Jimmy wasn't about to quit. I would have gotten out of bed and taken off down the hall if I could have. Having the opportunity to speak to a group of health care professionals would be as close as I would get to serving in that industry.

As I prepared for my presentation to the medical center staff, I talked about the customer service skills that are so important to giving great service to our customers and their patients. I tried to share many of the things as in this book that might make a difference to them in their personal and professional lives. No matter which career you choose, having good skills to interact with co-workers, management and customers, or in their case, patients, is important. The better job you do in the area of customer service, the more success you will enjoy.

One of the items I shared with that group is that having a heart of service is so important in the health care industry. When a health care provider sees a patient or a patient's family member, they may see them during a difficult time in the patient's life. The patient may be facing illness, financial hardships due to illness, fear, all the things that require a heart of service to properly deal with. That is why it was so important that I impress upon the health care providers that each employee really take that skill very seriously. A heart of service is important for each employee of that medical center. The doctors, the nurses, the registration staff, the kitchen staff, the janitorial staff, the security staff—the same heart of service is important.

The country doctor from my home town had that heart of service. He was a little rough on the staff members from the hospital, but he expected that heart of service from each team member. When Dr. Jimmy made his rounds, not only did he see his patients, he also stuck his head in the door of the other doctor's patients to see how they were doing. He wanted to make sure his hospital was taking good care of the customers. He loved the hospital and each patient there. In business we all need the heart of service that Dr. Jimmy had.

QUIET TIME

It is my opinion that everyone needs some quiet time. My quiet time is early morning, particularly Sunday morning. I report to the store at 7:30 in the morning. I get up at 5:30 or 6:00 am, depending on what I have going on for the day. I like to get up before anyone in the house. I will use a half an hour during the week and sometimes Sundays, more time. You see when it is quiet and there are no distractions, you can really think and concentrate. I use quiet time for all sorts of things. It makes a pretty good time to talk to the Lord, so sometimes a time for prayer is good for me. Sometimes I pray a thankful prayer, which for some reason seems to go a little quicker than the prayers where I need answers or those when I have problems and difficulties.

I have learned that life is that way. Just to say thank you goes quickly. Working through difficult situations, crises, problems and challenges takes a lot longer. I told you in an earlier chapter about the best salesmen I know. One was an alarm manufacturer executive and has now passed on. His name is Butch Work. He told me once that everyone we come in contact with is either coming out of some type of problem, in the middle of some type of problem or fixing to be in some type of problem. That being said, my quiet time is a good time to think out problems, identify, and come up with a solution to correct and work through them.

Being in business, I seem to have some type of issue that must be addressed each week—some are minor but some have the potential to become major without proper attention. Some company issues can be entirely delegated so my staff can learn to develop their quiet time and I let them hone their problem solving skills. Others I just need to handle. The point I am trying to make is, set aside quiet time because you are going to need it.

Sometimes, quiet time is Saturday afternoon after work. I get on my Harley and burn some octane. Just letting my mind rest for a little while and focusing on riding and nothing else seems to really do me good. Miss Kim usually will not ride the motorcycle with me. We have trailered it to Florida, and she will ride to supper or a day ride a little while we are down there, but she is not much on the local traffic.

One day a couple of years ago, I came in after a pretty challenging day. I don't even remember what was so challenging, but I had an attitude and Miss Kim didn't think it was a good attitude either. She said, "Look, Buddy, you need to get a shower, put on a pair of jeans and your boots, get that hot rod motorcycle out and twist that throttle and blow off a little steam, and work on that attitude." So I said, "Okay, let's go to Red Lobster and eat supper, I will wind it up a little and slow down then you can come by me in your truck and lead the way, because I always get lost around the mall." So we got on I-65 South and I twisted the throttle and got rolling pretty good. After a few minutes, I backed off and here she came. Man, she came by me in a hurry. When we got to Red Lobster, I said, "You let that Yukon roll didn't you?" She replied, "Yes, sometimes a girl has to blow off a little steam, too." I think it is important for everyone to find something that relaxes them and make time for that enjoyment. If not, burn out is most likely going to happen.

In the early spring I like to have a six week plan to get the yard, mulch and outdoor projects under way. So when motorcycle time is here, I am caught up on my honey-dos so I can ride. With the store hours Monday through Friday and a half day on Saturday, many outdoor projects cannot be finished on Saturday and will bleed in to Sunday morning. I give them a couple of hours and get ready for church. I try not to let my projects go in to the afternoon on Sunday so I can hang out with Miss Kim and rest for Monday.

If you are willing to help others, then you can always find help yourself.

When my parents were living, I would call them for advice when challenging times appeared. As I stated earlier, my mother had a special set of problem solving skills. Now they are gone and it seems like folks turn to me for problem solving. It is a huge honor, but many times the answers take time and even then I have to seek help from others. If you are willing to help others, then you can always find help yourself. Since my mother is gone, I sometimes call my sister Brenda to bounce ideas around. Getting her feedback seems to help me.

When I was young I enjoyed playing the guitar, riding motorcycles, being active in DeMolay, and working. Now that I'm older I have a renewed interest in motorcycles, guitars, and enjoy my work in Masonry. And of course I still enjoy my work.

The same pleasure and enjoyment I experienced doing those things as a teenager I get to experience again. Folks will often ask if I am still riding motorcycles. I still enjoy twisting the throttle just like I did when I was sixteen. I tell young people that if I were a little younger I would buy a fast sport motorcycle like the young folks ride. They usually reply, "Go Ahead!" Miss Kim said I should buy two of them, but I think I should stick to the big Harley baggers.

Everyone has challenges and has to come up with a plan of action that fits them to tackle those problems. For me, the things I mentioned in this quiet time section work best.

SOUTHERN LIVING

Growing up and living in the south is all I know. The farthest north I have ever driven was Louisville, Kentucky. I flew into Chicago one time on a diverted plane ride, but never got out of the terminal. I would like to visit our nation's capital and would like to see New York City someday. I have traveled in all three regions of Tennessee, west, middle and east, and have enjoyed its splendor, beauty and way of life. South Nashville is my home and I have no desire to live elsewhere. If you live in Nashville, you know what a special place it is. If you live elsewhere you need to visit.

Nashville has a little of everything you might want; great dinning, the finest of southern cooking at restaurants, and at just about every private dining table here, too. Any other cuisine your palate may desire, we've got that, too!

Just about every southern gal has a cornbread and fried chicken recipe, including Miss Kim. What a great cook!

This story I'm about tell you is probably just as suited for this section of the book as any, so here it goes. Many years ago Kim and I traveled to Boaz, Alabama on an overnight outlet mall shopping trip. While Kim was getting ready, I was watched a cooking show on cable TV. This was before the Food Network. I saw a recipe for ice box coconut cream pie. It seemed so simple; I knew I could make it. I didn't write it down, but put it in my memory for later use. A few years later, we were at the grocery store in the instant pudding section. I thought I would buy the ingredients and make some of those pies and give to some of my retired buddies. I bought instant pudding, graham cracker crusts, baker's coconut, milk, and whip topping. When we got home I asked Miss Kim for an apron, mixing bowl, measuring cup, and the electric mixer. I read the directions and started to mix my tasty concoction. I was spinning the bowl and really acting like a professional chef until I pulled out the mixer to look at the texture of my pie filling. You can't imagine the mess that makes when you don't take your thumb off the button. That sticky pudding mix was all over the ceiling, the counter, backsplash and all over Miss Kim. I finished my pies, delivered two of them and ate the other one. My two retired friends sure loved the pies, and when the word got out, I needed to make some more. The next week I went to Foodmax with Miss Kim and started putting boxes of pudding mix in our buggy, and Miss Kim said, "What do you think you are doing?" "I'm going to make some more pies," I said. "No, Mister. You just think you are!" she said.' Well it was years later and a new kitchen later before the pies were back on the menu. And I had to use a whisk.

Entertainment is abundant in Nashville as well; pro football, pro hockey, minor league baseball, college football, basketball, baseball, soccer, all types of athletics. We have night life. Our music venues are second to none, with the Nashville Symphony, Grand Ole Opry; Broadway plays at the Tennessee Performing Arts Center and of course, downtown honkey tonks. I'm so proud of our city and what we have to offer.

The best part of Nashville is our southern hospitality.

QUITTING AND GIVING UP

When our son Charlie was playing football in high school, he decided he was going to join the wrestling team. After a few matches he decided the sport was not for him. I told him he should not quit but should fulfill his commitment for the year. If he didn't want to wrestle the next year okay, but I didn't want him to quit until the year was done.

Earlier in the book I mentioned the story from Winston Churchill about the two frogs. The moral was to never give up. It has always been important to me to never be a quitter, and I taught my boys to never quit either. Just because something gets a little hard, don't quit.

We had a division in our company that started out as a profitable entity. It was hard work, and it had its share of aggravation, but it was an important part of our business for many years. We got to the point where it produced about $250,000 per year in revenue. Then some of our key accounts began to sell out or close. The serviceman we had running the truck was being courted by another company, so when the other portion of the company had to support that division, we decided to pull the plug and close that division. I struggled with that decision because I never like to lose or quit anything I start. But I learned that sometimes it makes sense to quit some endeavors.

In life and in business it is easy to get discouraged when challenges and obstacles arise. But I try to always stay motivated and never quit and give up. Being a little hard-headed seems to help us figure out ways to make things work.

Brad, Charlie, Amy, Miss Kim, myself and Langley at a Tennessee Titans game

DEVELOPING AND USING GOOD CUSTOMER SKILLS

When Miss Kim is cooking she often uses recipes written on index cards. When speaking to groups, I remind them that they already know the things I share with them. I just offer a few stories and analogies, so the skills will be like those recipes, easy to call on when needed.

Great customer skills are not learned overnight. I always remind our staff that good customer service is what customers expect and deserve. If we only give them good service, we haven't done anything special. But if we go to the next level and give them great service, we can out shine the competition and give them the wow factor. I tell our guys that what we do is important, but equally important is how we do it. I remind them that good body language is important; it shows confidence. Smiling when interacting with folks is very important. Always being a professional is important. Having the heart of service and a heart of sincerity is also important. Being compassionate, kind and patient is important. So is being a good listener. Good communications skills and good problem solving skills are so important. Properly resolving complaints quickly is so important. Knowing what your customers want and expect is important.

Coach Bryant used to talk about opportunity. Today we can give good customer service, but tomorrow we have the opportunity to give great customer service.

Each year we have friend day at church. Polls say 90% will come if asked. Ms. Kim invited one of the young families that trade with us to church. The young father was raised in Chicago and his wife was raised in Wisconsin, just outside of Green Bay. After church, we took them out to eat. After learning that Bonnie, the young wife, was a Packer fan, I asked if she had ever heard of Bart Starr. Not only had she heard of Bart Starr she had met him. I asked her to share her experience with us. She had been on a business trip to Birmingham. The chatter on the plane was that Bart Starr was on board. After the plane had landed, many people were gathered around Mr. Starr wanting to shake his hand and get an autograph. Bonnie didn't want to add to the mob so she gathered her belongings and started down the corridor. Here came a man walking very fast beside her—it was none other than Bart Starr. She increased her gait to keep up. She introduced herself to him and told him she, too, wanted an autograph but didn't want to hinder him with the crowd around him. He told Bonnie that there was a car waiting for him, and he didn't have time right then to stop and sign anything. But he reached in his coat pocket and gave her a business card. He instructed her to call his office and tell his assistant to send her as many autographed photos as she wanted.

He thanked Bonnie for being a fan and a supporter of the Packers.

After a few days Bonnie called his office and sure enough Mr. Starr's assistant told Bonnie she would put the pictures in the mail. Soon someone else wanted a picture, so Bonnie called to ask for one more. This time Bart Starr answered his phone. He remembered Bonnie and asked if she had gotten the pictures. She said she did and asked if it would be a bother to ask for one more. Bart Starr said it would not be a bother at all. He asked for her address and told her to call anytime. He said he was always accessible and was his pleasure to send as many pictures as she wanted.

I've never met Bart Starr personally, but I can tell he possesses a great love for people and has developed great customer service skills. No wonder he was so good on the field and after football in business.

I tell my staff the most important skill is to always thank our customers for the opportunity to serve them; and thank them for their business.

ALWAYS IMPACT WITH A POSITIVE INFLUENCE

Today I was positively influenced by our pastor's sermon. Dr. Mims spoke about hypocrisy. He talked about truth and the importance of leadership roles in church, family, and in business. In making a lot of presentations and trying to make a difference in people's lives and trying to share some of my knowledge, I forgot to mention perhaps the most important part of any relationship: trust. How could I forget to mention trust and honesty to the groups I speak to?

Sincerity and honesty leads to trust. Good leadership is important. Practice what you preach. Don't talk the talk and not walk the walk. My friend Bama Jim used to talk about walking the walk and talking the talk. He used to talk about other football teams that talked about beating Alabama. He would say, "Until you walk the walk, why talk the talk?"

Brother Gene Mims talked today about leaders. If leaders don't do a good job, how can they expect their followers to do a good job? He is right!

I feel the need to share part of that message today

with you. I want to be a good leader in my company and my family. When I wait on customers, I want them to have a feeling of trust and confidence in my recommendations to help them solve their car issues. I have had vehicles during the repair process that wound up not costing as much to repair, and that was a nice surprise to the customer. I have had others that had complications and cost more but I had to stick with the original estimate even after advising the customer during the repair process, because in the customer's mind it was the right thing to do. I have absorbed the difference many times just to keep down any friction or any problems at checkout time. Most companies would never do that. That is the reason it is so important to try to think ahead of any complications or cost differences that might occur. I would never let anyone doing work for me absorb cost differences when complications arose that were no fault of the individual. You see relationships have to be mutually beneficial.

Recently we did a strut mount replacement on a van. The customer's regular mechanic had replaced it while doing struts, but did not have the equipment to align the vehicle. When the client brought it to us for an alignment, it had a noise which was the mount. We replaced the mount and aligned the vehicle. Three months later the customer showed up without an appointment with her invoice in hand complaining of the mount noise.

I got her a ride home and replaced the mount at no charge and re-aligned the vehicle. There was no problem with the mount, but we felt it was necessary to ease her and her husband's minds. Two weeks later the husband called complaining of a vibration and wanted me to fix his problem. During our conversation, I learned that since I had seen the van last, he had purchased tires elsewhere and had his regular mechanic do some other work but wanted my expertise to go behind the other shops and make his problem go away. I told him that we had not been able to build a relationship since he was spending his money with other shops, and what work I had done I had to do twice just to try to make them happy. I could not see that relationship ever being mutually beneficial. I told him to go to the other people he had been trading with or expect to pay me for my diagnosis. He took offense to my direct approach. Trust is not a one way street. Sometimes the most profitable sale is the one you don't make. Thank goodness, most people will do the right thing and appreciate your efforts and be willing to be fair on their part of business transactions. Many times, years of experience will help to avoid problems and situations before they ever occur. I am so thankful for our regular and loyal customers. They make doing business such a delight.

One of our regulars, Ray Paley always brings us donuts when he gets his tires rotated.

Our regulars know about our great back up service and that our rotations after the sale are always at no charge, but they often ask if they owe anything. I appreciate their willingness to pay even when they don't owe. That makes up for the ones that might take advantage of my good nature sometimes.

Trust is an important thing. I had a friend tell me one time, "One hand don't clap." I see people handling situations much differently than I might handle them. I see folks in church that want everything the church and the church family can offer. But they don't give back. They don't try to lift anyone else up or try to be an encouragement to anyone else. They don't pray for anyone else. They don't offer financial assistance to help others and they don't tithe or give to special offerings.

To the givers and encouragers, may the Lord continue to bless you so you can give and encourage others. To the takers and discouragers, may the Lord continue to work on and move you. I hope to never be a non-giver or a non-encourager! If I do, I hope Miss Kim or my pastor or a friend will say, "What just happened here?"

As I get older, I find I need to plan more. I don't particularly like surprises. I like to plan my moves. Of course that is not always possible. I really like it when customers set up appointments for service and give me time to prepare for their visit. That doesn't happen very often, but when it does, it sure is nice. I like for vendors to call ahead before dropping in. That doesn't happen very often either. People like to plan from their schedules not yours.

Timing is important in business. But it is so important to make it as easy as possible for people to do business with you. So if it makes it easy for them, let them drop in!

CLOSING

Kim and I traveled today to my hometown of Dickson, Tennessee. My brother is traveling to New Orleans next week and I wanted to give him an autographed book by Retired Army General Boykin for him to read on his trip. My brother was an Army Ranger, and I thought he would enjoy the book. I also wanted to see a close friend, Kevin Rich, who lives in Dickson also.

I have mentioned several people by name that have influenced my life, both professionally and personally. These are only a tip of the iceberg. There are so many more that will read this book and say, "Steve, you need to tell about so and so." So many stories and my memory just can't remember all of them while I'm writing. Please don't be offended or feel slighted. Just write down your thoughts and I'll see about writing another book. All of my friends and customers are special. I wouldn't intentionally leave any one out.

Business has many twist turns and challenges. I have tried to tell about everyone I could think of. I have touched on many aspects of life and business. Always remember life occurs one step at a time. Tackle each challenge head on, one at a time. Always walk with the

Lord. Do your best. Do the right thing. Tough times don't last tough people do. Never give up. Always appreciate your family and friends. Perhaps the most important lesson in business is always, always thank your customer.

We will continually try our best to improve our system of doing business and change as times and customers change. The one thing that will never change is the way we treat our customers and friends. We will always give 110% and never forget what is important.

We all have a story to tell. I have enjoyed sharing my journey of life and business with you, *One Step At A Time.*

I hope my story will inspire, motivate, and encourage you. Thank you for reading my story. May the Lord bless you and your family, and we appreciate your business.

Steve Bass